Operational Paper P1
Management Accounting

Second edition 2015

ISBN 9781 4727 3436 5

e-Book ISBN 9781 4727 3658 1

British Library Cataloguing-in-Publication Data

A catalogue record for this book is available from the British Library

Published by

BPP Learning Media Ltd,
BPP House, Aldine Place,
142-144 Uxbridge Road,
London W12 8AA

www.bpp.com/learningmedia

Printed in the United Kingdom by Ashford

Unit 600
Fareham Reach
Gosport
Hampshire
PO13 0FW

Welcome to BPP Learning Media's CIMA **Passcards** for Operational **Paper P1 Management Accounting**.

- They **focus on your exam** and **save you time**.

- They incorporate **diagrams** to kick start your memory.

- They follow the overall **structure** of the BPP Learning Media Study Texts, but BPP Learning Media's CIMA **Passcards** are not just a condensed book. Each card has been separately designed for clear presentation. Topics are self contained and can be grasped visually.

- CIMA **Passcards** are still **just the right size** for pockets, briefcases and bags.

Run through the **Passcards** as often as you can during your final revision period. The day before the exam, try to go through the **Passcards** again! You will then be well on your way to passing your exams.

Good luck!

Contents

1: Modern business concepts

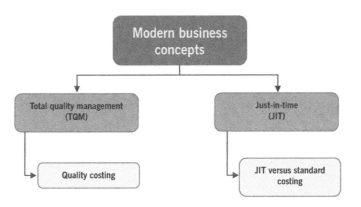

Changing competitive environment

	Then	Now
Manufacturing organisations	Pre 1970s, there was little overseas competition, costs were passed on to customers, minimal efforts were made to maximise efficiency/reduce costs/improve management practices.	There is massive overseas competition, and global networks for acquiring raw materials and distributing high quality, low-priced goods.
Service organisations	Pre 1980s, many were government-owned monopolies or protected by highly regulated, non-competitive environments. Cost increases were covered by increasing prices. Cost systems were not deemed necessary.	Privatisation and deregulation has resulted in intense competition, an increasing product range and a need for sophisticated costing systems.
Product life cycles	Organisations could rely on years of high demand for products.	Competitive environment, technological innovation and discriminating and sophisticated customer demand require continual product redesign and quick time to market.

Changing customer requirements

Successful organisations make customer satisfaction their priority.

Key success factors
■ Cost efficiency
■ Quality
■ Time
■ Innovation

New management approaches
■ Continuous improvement
■ Employee empowerment
■ Total value chain analysis

Changing manufacturing systems

Traditional manufacturing systems
■ Jobbing industries
■ Batch processing
■ Mass/flow production

Recent developments
■ Group technology/repetitive manufacturing
■ Dedicated cell layout

Manufacturing processes must be sufficiently flexible both to accommodate new product design and to satisfy the demand for greater product diversity.

Computer-aided design (CAD)

- The effects of changing product specifications can be explored.
- Designs can be assessed in terms of cost and simplicity.
- Databases can match required and existing parts to reduce parts required and minimise inventory holdings.

Flexible manufacturing systems (FMS)

- An FMS is a highly automated manufacturing system characterised by small batch production, the ability to change quickly from one job to another and very fast response times.
- Features include just in time (JIT) systems, computer integrated manufacturing (CIM), computerised materials handling systems (MHS) and automated storage and retrieval systems (ASRs).

Computer-aided manufacturing (CAM)

- CAM includes robots, CNC machines, AGVs and ASRs.
- The ultimate aim is a set-up time of zero.
- It allows production in very small batch sizes (so that the production schedule is driven by customer requirements).

Electronic data interchange (EDI)

EDI facilitates communications between an organisation and its customers/suppliers by electronic transfer of information.

Traditional responses to the problems of improving manufacturing capacity and reducing unit costs of production

- Longer production runs
- Economic batch quantities
- Fewer products in the product range
- More overtime
- Reduced time on preventative maintenance, to keep production flowing

Just-in-time systems challenge such 'traditional' views.

Although often described as a technique, JIT is more of a philosophy since it encompasses a commitment to continuous improvement and a search for excellence in the design and operation of the production management system.

Aims of JIT

- Minimise warehousing and storage costs.

- Eliminate waste by maintaining control over quality of inventory input to the production process.

- Reduce the amount of raw materials and WIP carried as working capital through more effective production planning.

- Reduce the amount of finished goods held as working capital.

1: Modern business concepts

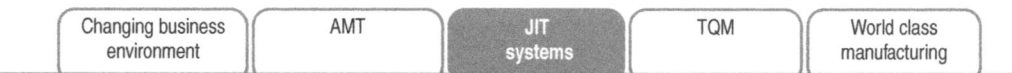

Essential elements of JIT

- JIT purchasing
- Close relationships with suppliers
- Uniform loading
- Set-up time reduction
- Machine cells

- Quality
- Pull system (Kanban)
- Preventative maintenance
- Employee involvement
- Elimination of non-value-added costs

Problems with JIT

- Can be difficult to predict patterns of demand
- Makes the organisation vulnerable to disruptions in the supply chain
- Wide geographical spread makes its operation difficult

Value-added costs

Incurred for an activity that cannot be eliminated without the customer perceiving a deterioration in the performance, function or other quality of a product

Value is only added while a product is actually being processed.

Total Quality Management (TQM)

The process of focusing on quality in the management of *all* resources and relationships within the organisation

Two basic principles of TQM

Getting things right first time, on the basis that the cost of correcting mistakes is greater than the cost of preventing them from happening in the first place

Continuous improvement – the belief that it is always possible to improve, no matter how high quality may be already

Measuring and controlling quality

1 **Quality assurance** (supplier guarantees quality)

2 **Inspection of output** (at various key stages)

3 **Monitoring customer reaction** (involves monitoring complaints in the form of letters, returned goods, requests for servicing and so on)

Employees and quality

- Workers are **empowered** and encouraged to become **multiskilled.**

- Workers are encouraged to **take responsibility** for their work.

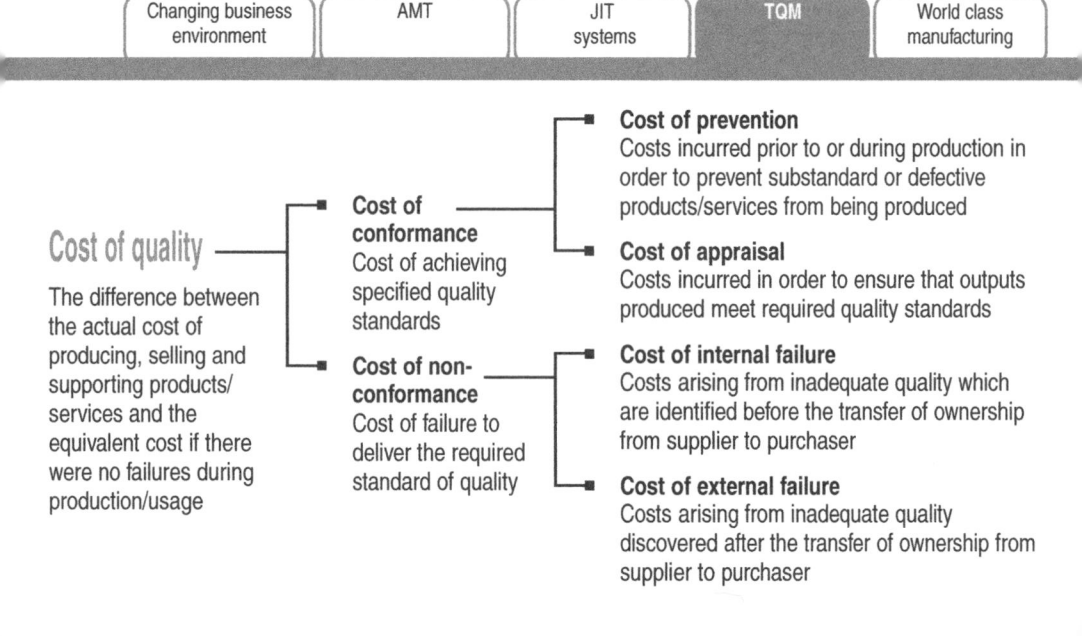

Cost of quality

The difference between the actual cost of producing, selling and supporting products/services and the equivalent cost if there were no failures during production/usage

Cost of conformance
Cost of achieving specified quality standards

Cost of prevention
Costs incurred prior to or during production in order to prevent substandard or defective products/services from being produced

Cost of appraisal
Costs incurred in order to ensure that outputs produced meet required quality standards

Cost of non-conformance
Cost of failure to deliver the required standard of quality

Cost of internal failure
Costs arising from inadequate quality which are identified before the transfer of ownership from supplier to purchaser

Cost of external failure
Costs arising from inadequate quality discovered after the transfer of ownership from supplier to purchaser

The cost of conformance is a discretionary cost incurred with the intention of eliminating non-conformance costs. The cost of non-conformance can only be reduced by increasing the cost of conformance. The optimal investment in conformance costs is when total costs of quality reach a minimum (which may be below 100% quality conformance).

Examples

Cost of prevention	**Cost of appraisal**	**Cost of internal failure**	**Cost of external failure**
Training in quality control	Inspection of goods inwards	Losses due to lower selling prices for sub-quality goods	Cost of customer service section

Cost of quality reports

Such reports show how much is being spent on each of the categories.

They indicate how total cost can be reduced by more sensible division of costs between the categories.

Non-financial measures (eg number of warranty claims) may be more appropriate for lower-level managers.

World Class Manufacturing (WCM)

'The manufacture of high-quality products reaching customers quickly (or the delivery of a prompt and quality service) at a low cost to provide high performance and customer satisfaction.' *(Clarke)*

Key elements of WCM

- Achieving 100% quality
- JIT manufacturing
- Managing people (multiskilling, teamwork, empowerment)
- Response to customers (knowing their requirements, supplying on time, responding to changes in needs)

2: Environmental costing

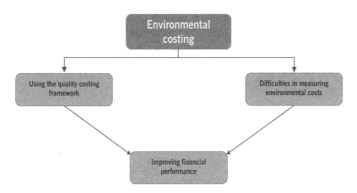

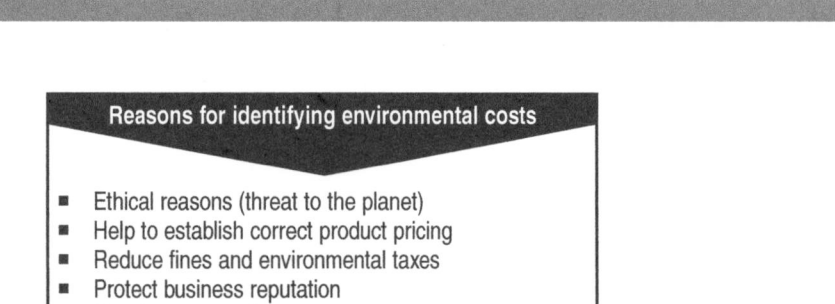

Reasons for identifying environmental costs

- Ethical reasons (threat to the planet)
- Help to establish correct product pricing
- Reduce fines and environmental taxes
- Protect business reputation
- Regulatory compliance
- General cost savings (for example, energy)

Businesses may suffer significant costs and loss of reputation if problems arise.

Environmental footprint

This is the impact that a business's activities have upon the environment including its resource environment and pollution emissions.

Carbon trading

Businesses that emit less than their allowance are able to sell the right to emit CO_2 to another business.

UNFCCC

United Nations Framework Convention on Climate Change agreements:

External impacts

- Depletion of natural resources
- Noise and aesthetic impacts
- Residual air and water emissions
- Long-term waste disposal
- Health effects
- Change in local quality of life

- To develop programmes to slow climate change

- To share technology and co-operate to reduce greenhouse gas emissions

- To develop a greenhouse gas inventory listing national sources and carbon sinks

2: Environmental costing

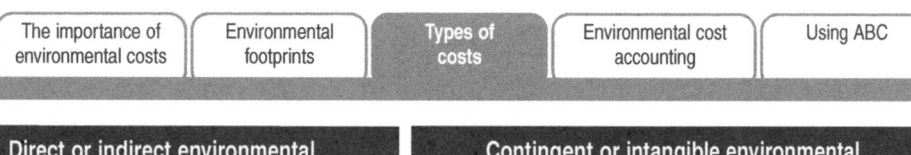

Direct or indirect environmental costs

- Waste management
- Remediation costs
- Permits, legal costs and fines
- Environmental certification
- Record keeping and reporting

Contingent or intangible environmental costs

- Uncertain future remediation or compensation costs
- Product quality
- Employee health and safety
- Public/customer perception
- Sustainability of raw material inputs

Environmental prevention costs – costs required to eliminate impacts before they occur

– eg forming environmental policies

Environmental appraisal costs – costs involved in establishing whether activities comply to environmental policies

– eg costs of monitoring, testing and inspection

Internal failure costs

Costs of activities that must be undertaken when contaminants and waste have been created by a business but not released into the environment.

Eg maintaining pollution equipment.

External failure costs

Costs which arise when a business releases harmful waste into the environment.

Eg cleaning up an oil spill.

Environmental policy

This may include reduction/management of risk to the business, motivating staff and enhancement of reputation.

ISO 14001 prescribes that an environmental management system must comprise:

- An environmental policy statement
- An assessment of environmental aspects and legal and voluntary obligations
- A management system
- Internal audits and reports to senior management
- A public declaration that ISO 14001 is being complied with

It has been suggested that businesses should pay for external environmental costs.

Environmental cost accounting

This involves establishing the real costs that businesses incur by internalising external environmental costs.

This means adding costs which the business would need to incur to reduce the impacts of environmental damage or to restore damage done.

These costs are deducted from profit to give a sustainable profit.

Estimating sustainable profits

1 Decide on areas where environmental costs can be controlled

2 Establish targets

3 Identify impact business has on the environment

4 Calculate what the business needs to spend to avoid impacts or restore damage

Traditional management accounting systems fail to analyse environmental costs. Costs such as energy and water become hidden within production overheads.

Using ABC, environmental costs become cost drivers.

Life cycle costing

Consideration of the costs throughout a product's life is known as the life cycle costing approach. Environmental costs should be considered using this approach, particularly as some end-of-life costs may be significant.

Consider

- Volume of emissions/waste
- How toxic emissions are
- Relative cost of treating different emissions

Benefits

- Costs become more visible
- Potential future costs may be prevented or reduced before they occur

3: Absorption and activity based costing

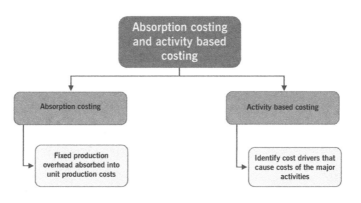

Basic principles of cost behaviour and cost behaviour patterns

Cost behaviour is the variability of costs with activity undertaken. The basic principle of cost behaviour is that as the level of activity rises, costs will usually rise.

Fixed costs

Fixed costs are not affected by the level of activity.

Step costs

Step costs are fixed in nature but only within certain levels of activity.

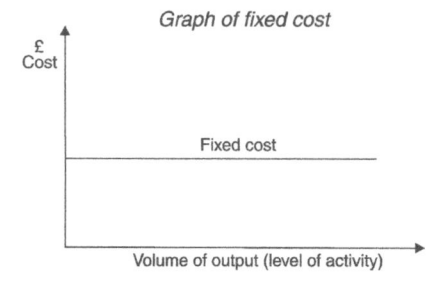

Graph of fixed cost

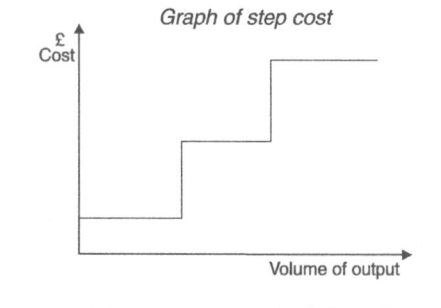

Graph of step cost

Variable costs

Variable costs increase or decrease with the level of activity.

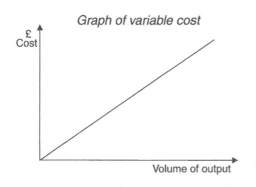

Graph of variable cost

Non-linear variable costs

Although variable costs are usually assumed to be linear, there are situations where variable costs are curvilinear as shown in the following graphs.

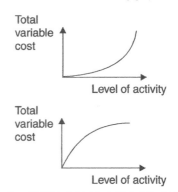

Semi-variable costs (or semi-fixed costs or mixed costs)

Semi variable/semi-fixed or mixed costs are costs which are part-fixed and part-variable. This means that they are partly affected by a change in the level of activity.

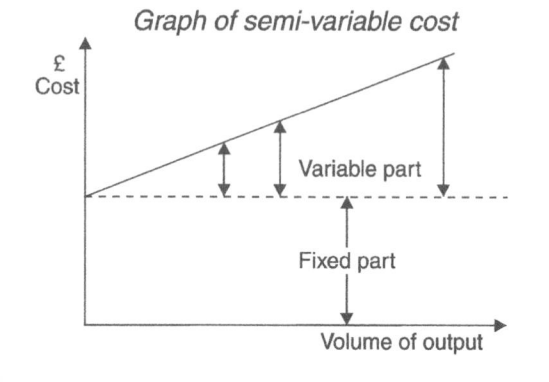

Graph of semi-variable cost

Examples of semi-variable costs

Electricity and gas bills where there is a basic charge plus a charge per unit of consumption

A sales representative's salary where a basic monthly amount is supplemented by commission on the value of sales made

Determining the fixed and variable elements of semi-variable costs

The fixed and variable elements of semi-variable costs can be determined by the **high-low method**.

> ### High-low method
>
> The two periods with the **highest** and **lowest** volumes of activity are selected.
> The difference between the total cost of these two periods is the **variable cost** of the difference in activity levels (since the same fixed cost is included in each total cost).
>
> The variable cost per unit may be calculated from this (difference in total costs ÷ difference in activity levels).
>
> The **fixed cost** may then be determined by substitution.

1 Allocation

Process by which whole cost items are charged *direct* to a cost unit or cost centre (without the need for apportionment).

2 Apportionment

First stage involves 'sharing out' overheads in general overhead cost centres (eg rent and rates) between the other cost centres using a fair basis (such as floor area occupied by each cost centre for rent and rates).

Second stage involves sharing out the (directly allocated and apportioned) costs within service cost centres to production cost centres.

3 Absorption

> Overhead absorption rate (OAR) = estimated overhead ÷ budgeted activity level

Example

Budgeted overhead: £100,000
Budgeted labour cost: £200,000 for 20,000 hrs
Budgeted output: 2,000 units
OARs: £50 per unit
Actual overhead: £110,000
Actual output: 1,800 units

	£
Actual overhead	110,000
O/hd absorbed (1,800 × £50)	90,000
Under-absorbed overhead	20,000

Under/over absorption occurs because overhead absorbed is based on estimated expenditure and activity levels.

Under/over absorption

- O/hd incurred > o/hd absorbed ⇒ under-absorbed o/hd = adverse adjustment to income statement

- O/hd incurred < o/hd absorbed ⇒ over-absorbed o/hd = favourable adjustment to income statement

Inventories are valued at their full production cost including absorbed fixed production costs.

Modern manufacturing environment

- An increase in support services (such as production scheduling)

  - These services assist in the manufacture of a wide range of products.

  - They are unaffected by changes in production volume.

  - They vary instead with the range and complexity of products.

- An increase in overheads as a proportion of total costs

Inadequacies of absorption costing

- Implies all overheads are related to production volume

- Developed at a time when organisations produced only a narrow range of products and when overheads were only a small fraction of total costs

- Tends to allocate too great a proportion of overheads to high-volume products (which cause relatively little diversity) and too small a proportion to low-volume products (which cause greater diversity and use more support services)

Outline of an ABC system

1. Identify an organisation's major activities. (Activities cause costs.)

2. Identify **cost drivers**. ◼

3. Collect the costs associated with each activity into **cost pools**.

4. Charge costs of each cost pool to products on the basis of products' usage of the activity (measured by number of the activity's cost driver a product generates) using a cost driver rate (total costs in cost pool ÷ total number of cost drivers).

Cost drivers

Any factor which causes a change in the cost of an activity

Examples

The cost driver for a cost that varies with production volume in the short term (such as power costs) should be volume related (eg labour hours or machine hours).

The cost driver for a cost that is related to the transactions undertaken by the support department where the cost is incurred should be the transaction in the support department (such as the number of production runs for the cost of setting up production runs).

Example

Cost of goods inwards department totalled £10,000. Cost driver for goods inwards activity is number of deliveries. During 20X0 there were 1,000 deliveries. 200 of these deliveries related to product X. 2,000 units of product X were produced.

Cost per unit of cost driver
$$= £10,000/1,000$$
$$= £10$$

Cost of activity attributable to product X
$$= £10 \times 200$$
$$= £2,000$$

Cost of activity per unit of product X
$$= £2,000/2,000$$
$$= £1$$

When should ABC be introduced?

If the additional information it provides results in action that increases organisational profitability.

This will tend to occur if:

- production overheads are high in relation to direct costs (especially labour),

- overhead resource consumption is not just driven by production volume,

- there is wide variety in the product range, *or*

- overhead resource input varies significantly across the product range

Transactions analysis

Logistical transactions Activities concerned with organising the flow of resources throughout the manufacturing process

Balancing transactions Activities which ensure that demand for and supply of resources are matched

Quality transactions Activities which relate to ensuring that production is at the required level of quality

Change transactions Activities associated with ensuring that customers' requirements are met

The primary driver of these activities (which cause overheads to be incurred) is not normally production volume.

Analysis of activities

Costs of...	such as...	are dependent on...
Unit level activities	machine power	volume of production
Batch level activities	set-up costs	number of batches
Product level activities	product management	existence of a product group/line
Facility level activities	rent and rates	organisation simply being in business

If most overheads are related to unit level/facility level activities, costs determined using ABC and absorption costing will be similar. If overheads are associated with batch/product level activities, however, they will be significantly different.

Merits	Criticisms
☑ Simple (once information is obtained)	☒ ABC is more complex than absorption costing and so should only be introduced if it provides additional management information
☑ Recognises the complexity of modern manufacturing with its multiple cost drivers	☒ Cost drivers might be difficult to identify
☑ Facilitates a good understanding of what drives overhead costs	☒ Can one cost driver explain the behaviour of all items in a cost pool?
☑ Concerned not just with production costs but *all* overhead costs	☒ Some measure of arbitrary cost apportionment is still needed for costs such as rent and rates
☑ Helps with cost control (because by controlling the incidence of the cost driver, the level of cost can be controlled)	
☑ Can help with cost management	
☑ Can be used in conjunction with customer profitability analysis	

4: Marginal and throughput accounting

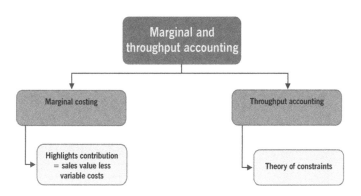

Three major principles

1 Variable costs are charged to the cost of making/selling a product, fixed costs are charged direct to the income statement.

2 Inventory is valued at variable production cost (not full production cost as with absorption costing).

3 Profit = total contribution (difference between sales revenue and *all* variable costs) – period fixed costs.

If the opening and closing inventory values differ, the difference in profits using the two methods equals the difference in the fixed overhead included in the absorption costing opening and closing inventory valuations (see page 14).

In the long run, profit is the same whatever method is used.

Profit statements

Absorption costing

	£	£
Turnover		X
Opening inventory (at full cost)	X	
Full prod'n costs (var + abs'd fixed o/hd)	X	
Less closing inventory (at full cost)	X	
Production cost of sales	X	
Under/over-absorbed overhead	X	
Total costs		X
Gross profit		X
Other costs		X
Net profit		X

Marginal costing

	£	£
Turnover		X
Opening inventory (at variable cost)	X	
Variable production costs	X	
Less closing inventory (at variable cost)	X	
Variable prod'n cost of sales		X
Contribution		X
Fixed costs		X
Profit		X

Reconciling profit figures

The figures given by the two methods	
	£
Marginal costing profit	X
Adjust for fixed overhead in inventory	
+ Inventory increase in units × fixed overhead absorbed per unit OR	X
– Inventory decrease in units × fixed overhead absorbed per unit	
Absorption costing profit	X

If the opening inventory volumes are greater than closing inventory volumes, marginal costing shows the greater profit.

Example

Opening inventory: 100 units

Closing inventory: 195 units

Fixed OAR = £17 per unit

Marginal costing profit = £73,500

Absorption costing profit is therefore higher and equals £73,500 + ((195 – 100) × £17) = £75,115

Arguments in favour of absorption costing	Arguments in favour of marginal costing
■ When sales fluctuate because of seasonality in sales demand but production is held constant, absorption costing avoids large fluctuations in profit.	■ It shows how an organisation's cash flows and profits are affected by changes in sales volumes since contribution varies in direct proportion to units sold.
■ Marginal costing fails to recognise the importance of working to full capacity and its effects on pricing decisions if a cost plus method of pricing is being used.	■ By using absorption costing and setting a production level greater than sales demand, profits can be manipulated.
■ Prices based on marginal cost (minimum prices) do not guarantee that contribution will cover fixed costs.	■ Separating fixed and variable costs is vital for decision making.
■ In the long run all costs are variable, and absorption costing recognises these long-run variable costs.	■ For short-run decisions in which fixed costs do not change (such as short-run tactical decisions seeking to make the best use of existing resources), the decision rule is to choose the alternative which maximises *contribution*, fixed costs being irrelevant.
■ It is consistent with the requirements of IAS 2.	

Full cost-plus pricing

The sales price is determined by calculating the full cost of the product and then adding a % mark-up for profit.

- An average profit mark-up can be used as a general guideline if prices must be quoted regularly to prospective customers.

- The mark-up does not have to be rigid and fixed but can be varied to suit the circumstances.

- Quick, simple and cheap method of pricing.

Problems

- The price must be adjusted to suit market and demand conditions.

- Output volume (a key factor in the determination of the overhead absorption rate) has to be budgeted.

- Suitable overhead absorption bases must be selected.

- Most importantly, full cost plus pricing fails to recognise that since demand may be determined by price, there will be a profit-maximising combination of price and demand.

A full cost determined by activity based costing as opposed to absorption costing might be more appropriate in today's business environment.

Marginal cost-plus pricing / mark-up pricing

Sales price = marginal cost of production (or marginal cost of sales) + profit margin

Pricing in a limiting factor situation

Suppose a business is working at full capacity and is restricted by a shortage of resources from expanding its output further. By deciding what target profit it would like to earn, it can establish a mark-up per unit of limiting factor.

Advantages of mark-up pricing

- ☑ Simple and easy
- ☑ Mark-up percentage can be varied to reflect demand conditions
- ☑ Helps create a better awareness of the concepts and implications of marginal cost and CVP analysis
- ☑ Used by businesses where there is a readily-identifiable basic variable cost (eg retail industries)

Drawbacks of mark-up pricing

- ☒ Does not ensure that sufficient attention is paid to demand conditions, competitors' prices and profit maximisation
- ☒ Ignores fixed overheads

Theory of constraints (TOC)

An **approach to production management** which aims to maximise sales revenue less material and variable overhead costs. It focuses on the factors which act as constraints to this maximisation.

Binding constraint

A process that acts as a bottleneck (or limiting factor) and constrains throughput.

Principles

Inventory costs money in terms of storage space and interest and so is undesirable.

The only inventory that should be held is a buffer inventory immediately prior to the bottleneck so that output through it is never held up.

Operations prior to the binding constraint should operate at the same speed as the binding constraint otherwise WIP will build up.

Aim

Maximise **throughput contribution** (sales revenue less material cost) while keeping **conversion costs** (all operating costs except material cost) and **investment costs** (inventory, equipment, building costs etc) to a minimum.

TOC is not an accounting system. It is a production system.

Throughput accounting (TA)

An **approach to accounting**, in line with the JIT philosophy, which assumes management have a given set of resources available (existing buildings, capital equipment, labour force). Using these resources, purchased materials and parts must be processed to generate sales revenue. The most appropriate financial objective to set is therefore maximisation of throughput (sales revenue less direct material cost).

Why is TA different?

TA differs from other accounting systems because of what it **emphasises**.

1. **Throughput**

2. **Inventory minimisation**

3. **Cost control**

Examples

Throughput accounting can be used successfully in service and retail industries.

If there is a delay in processing a potential customer's application, business can be lost.

A bottleneck might form if work that could be done by nurses has to be carried out by doctors.

4: Marginal and throughput accounting

Three concepts upon which TA is based

1. All factory costs except materials costs are fixed.

2. The ideal inventory level is zero (apart from a buffer inventory prior to the bottleneck) and so unavoidable idle capacity is inevitable.

3. No value is added and no profit is made until a sale takes place.

Factors that limit throughput

- Bottleneck resources
- Lack of product quality/reliability
- Unreliable material supplies
- Customers with particular demands

Throughput measures

- **Return per time period***

  Throughput contribution ÷ time period

- **Return per time period on bottleneck resource***

  Throughput contribution ÷ minutes (say) on bottleneck resource

- **TA ratio***

  Throughput contribution per time period ÷ conversion cost (ie labour + o/head) per time period

- **Current effectiveness ratio**

  Standard minutes of throughput achieved ÷ minutes available

  * Based on **throughput contribution** or **return** or **value added** = sales – material costs

Criticisms	Advantages

Criticisms

- It is seen by some as too short term, as all costs other than direct material cost are regarded as fixed.
- It concentrates on direct material cost and does not control other costs.
- By attempting to maximise throughput an organisation could be producing in excess of profit-maximising output.

Advantages

The principal advantage of TA is that it directs attention to critical factors.

- Bottlenecks
- Key elements in making profit
- Inventory reduction
- Reducing response time to customer demand
- Even production flow
- Overall effectiveness and efficiency

Notes

5: Limiting factor analysis

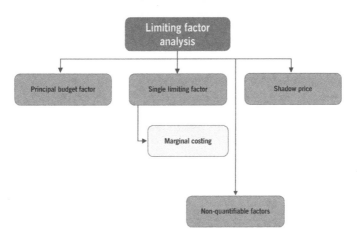

Scenario

Sales demand restricts greater production/output

One scarce resource (such as material or labour)

One limiting factor and restrictions on sales demand or two potentially limiting factors

How to maximise contribution/profit

Make exactly the amount required for sales (and no more) provided that each product sold earns a positive contribution.

Earn the biggest possible contribution per unit of scarce resource (see example below).

Rank products in order of contribution-earning ability per unit of limiting factor but produce the top-ranked products up to the sales demand limit.

Detail

Assume fixed costs remain unchanged whatever the production mix, the only relevant costs being variable costs.

Although there may appear to be more than one scarce resource, it may be that there is no limiting factor except sales demand or that there is only one scarce resource that prevents full potential sales demand being achieved.

If you suspect the existence of a limiting factor, some quick computations should confirm your suspicions.

1 Calculate the amount of the scarce resource (material quantities, labour hours, machine hours and so on) needed to meet the potential sales demand.

2 Calculate the amount of the scarce resource available (for example number of employees multiplied by maximum working hours per employee).

3 Compare the two figures. Obviously, if the resources needed exceed the resources available, there is a limiting factor on output and sales.

Example

L Co sells two products, the T and the J.

	T	J
	£	£
Direct labour (£5 per hour)	15	10
Direct materials (£2 per kg)	2	5
Variable overheads	2	2
Fixed overheads	3	3
	22	20
Selling price	£25	£24
Maximum demand	10,000	8,000
Maximum availability of labour		40,000 hrs

1 Confirm limiting factor is *not* sales.

Labour hours required to fulfil demand = $(10,000 \times 3) + (8,000 \times 2) = 46,000$, which means there is a shortfall of 6,000 hours.

2 Calculate the contribution per unit of scarce resource.

	T	J
Unit contribution	£(25 – 19) £6	£(24 – 17) £7
Labour hours per unit	3	2
Contribution per labour hour	£2	£3.50
Rank	2nd	1st

3 Work out budgeted production and sales.

Product	Hours	Production	Cont'n per unit £	Total cont'n £
J	(8,000 × 2) = 16,000	(÷ 2) 8,000	7	56,000
T	Balance = 24,000	(÷ 3) 8,000	6	48,000
	40,000			104,000

The profit-maximising product mix might not be possible because the mix is also restricted by a factor other than a scarce resource.

In such circumstances the organisation might have to produce more of a particular product or products than the level established by ranking according to contribution per unit of limiting factor.

Factors that restrict freedom of action

- A contract to supply a certain number of products
- Provision of a complete product range and/or maintenance of customer goodwill
- Maintenance of a certain market share

Basic approach

1 Rank the products in the normal way.

2 Take account of the minimum production requirements within the optimum production plan.

3 Allocate the remaining resources according to the ranking.

Example

In the earlier example about L Co, suppose that the company has contracted to supply 9,000 units of T to an important customer. Here is the revised optimum sales/production plan.

Product	Hours	Production	Contribution per unit £	Total contribution £
T	(9,000 × 3) = 27,000	9,000	6	54,000
J	balance = 13,000	(13,000 ÷ 2) = 6,500	7	45,500
	40,000			99,500

An examination question is highly unlikely to tell you that an organisation has a 'restricted freedom of action'. Instead, look out for hints such as 'contracted to supply ...', 'minimum to be produced ...' and so on.

Suppose a company must subcontract work to make up a shortfall in its own production capacity.

Its total costs are minimised if those units bought have the lowest extra variable cost of buying per unit of scarce resource saved.

Example

A company, which makes three products, has limited labour time available.

	A	B	C
	£	£	£
Variable cost of making	10	16	14
Variable cost of buying	19	20	19
Extra variable cost of buying	9	4	5
Labour hours saved by buying (per unit)	3	2	2
Extra variable cost of buying per hour saved	£3	£2	£2.50
Priority for making in-house	1st	3rd	2nd

Opportunity cost

This represents the benefits foregone by using a limiting factor in one way instead of the next most profitable way.

Example (L Co)

In the example earlier, the opportunity cost of making J instead of more units of T is £2 per labour hour (T's contribution per labour hour).

If more labour hours were made available, more units of T (up to 10,000) would be made and an extra contribution of £2 per labour hour could be earned.

Similarly if fewer labour hours were available, fewer units of T would be made, production of J being kept at 8,000 units.

The loss of labour hours would cost the company £2 per labour hour in lost contribution. ▪

Shadow price (dual price)

A shadow price is the increase in contribution which would be created by having available one additional unit of a limiting resource at its normal variable cost.

This **lost contribution** (which is the marginal-earning potential of the limiting factor at the profit-maximising output level), is the **internal opportunity cost** or **shadow price** (or **dual price**) of the limiting factor.

Assumptions in limiting factor analysis

- Fixed costs will be the same whatever decision is taken.
- Unit variable costs are constant for all quantities of output.
- Sales demand is known with certainty.
- Resource requirements are known with certainty.
- Units of output are divisible.

Further considerations

- How much will sales demand be affected by changes in sales price, and how interdependent are sales of different products?
- Customer loyalty may be adversely affected by the business ceasing to produce a product.
- Competitors may take over vacated markets.
- It may not be possible to restart production of the product if labour skills have been lost.
- Further research may indicate the limiting factor is only limiting because of problems with the production process.
- Managers may want to achieve a satisfactory mix rather than a profit-maximising product mix in order to maintain employee goodwill.

6: Relevant costs

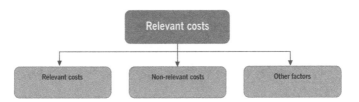

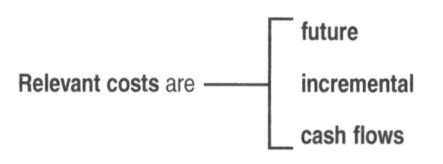

Relevant costs are —— future / incremental / cash flows

Examples

Avoidable costs are costs which would not be incurred if the activity to which they relate did not exist.

A **differential cost** is the difference in total costs between alternatives.

An **opportunity cost** is the benefit which would have been earned, but which has been given up, by choosing one option instead of another.

The relevance of fixed costs

- **Directly attributable fixed costs**, although fixed within a relevant range or regarded as fixed because management has set a budgeted expenditure level, are relevant because they do one of two things.

  - Increase if certain activities are undertaken
  - Decrease/are eliminated if a decision is taken to reduce the scale of operations/shutdown entirely

- **General fixed overheads** (such as an apportioned share of head office charges) are unaffected by a change in the scale of operations and are irrelevant.

Non-relevant costs

Cost	Description	Example
Sunk costs	Expenditure which has already been incurred and charged, or which has already been incurred or which which relates to an expenditure decision which has irrevocably been taken, and which will be charged in a future accounting period	**Development costs already incurred**
Committed costs	Future cash outflows that will be incurred regardless of the decision taken	**Contracts already entered into**
Notional costs	Hypothetical accounting costs which reflect the use of a benefit for which no actual cash expense is incurred	**Notional rent**
Historical costs	Will often provide the best available basis for predicting future costs	**Lease payments**

Relevant cost of materials

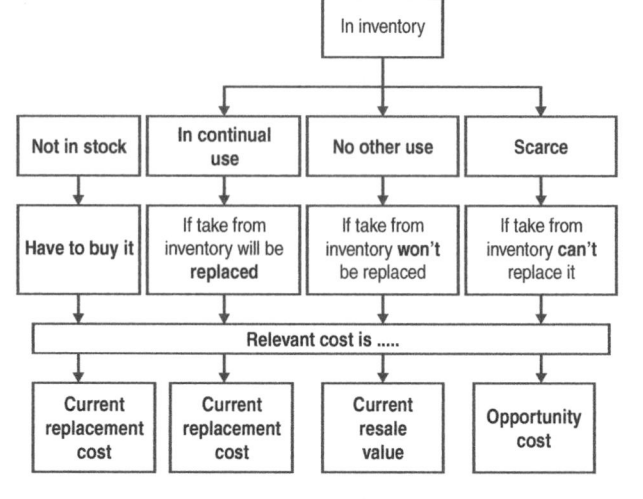

Relevant cost of labour and variable overheads

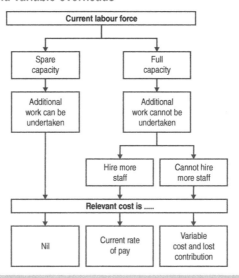

Relevant cost of using machines

- Repair costs
- Hire charges
- Fall in resale value of owned assets resulting from their use

Depreciation is not a relevant cost

Relevant cost of a scarce resource = contribution/incremental profit forgone from the next best opportunity for using the scarce resource (**opportunity cost**) + variable cost of the scarce resource (cash expenditure to purchase it, if it has not already been purchased)

Remember, relevant revenues are also future, incremental cash flows.

Assumptions in relevant costing

1 Cost behaviour patterns are known.

2 The amount of fixed costs, unit variable costs, sales price and sales demand are known with certainty.

3 The objective of decision making in the short term is to maximise 'satisfaction', which is often regarded as 'short-term profit'.

4 The information on which a decision is based is complete and reliable.

For once-only decisions, or decisions affecting the use of marginal spare capacity, absorption costing information about unit profits is irrelevant and misleading.

Non-quantifiable factors in decision making

- The availability of cash
- Employees
- Customers
- Competitors
- Timing factors
- Suppliers
- Feasibility
- Flexibility and internal control
- Unquantified opportunity costs
- Political pressures
- Legal constraints
- Inflation

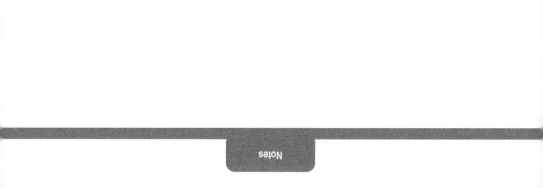

Notes

7: Multi-product breakeven analysis

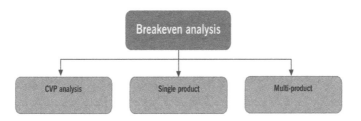

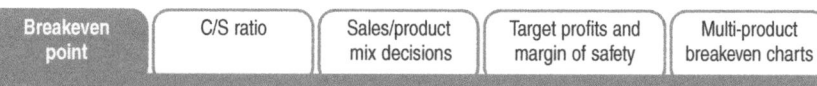

| Breakeven point | C/S ratio | Sales/product mix decisions | Target profits and margin of safety | Multi-product breakeven charts |

Example (J Co) used throughout this chapter (where appropriate)

J Co produces and sells two products

- The M sells for £7 per unit and has a total variable cost of £3 per unit.
- The N sells for £15 per unit an.d has a total variable cost of £5 per unit.

For every five units of M sold, one unit of N will be sold.

Fixed costs total £30,000.

How to calculate a multi-product breakeven point

1. Calculate the contribution per unit.
2. Calculate the contribution per mix.
3. Calculate the breakeven point in number of mixes.
4. Calculate the breakeven point in units and revenue.

Example (J Co)

1. M = £4   N = £10
2. (£4 × 5) + (£10 × 1) = £30
3. Fixed costs ÷ contribution per mix = £30,000 ÷ £30
   = 1,000 mixes
4. M   1,000 × 5 = 5,000 units
       5,000 × £7 = £35,000 revenue

   N   1,000 × 1 = 1,000 units
       1,000 × £15 = £15,000 revenue

   Total breakeven revenue = £50,000

How to calculate a multi-product C/S (or profit volume or P/V) ratio

Calculation of breakeven sales: approach 1

1 Calculate the revenue per mix.

2 Calculate the contribution per mix.

3 Calculate the average C/S ratio.

4 Calculate the total breakeven point.

5 Calculate the revenue ratio per mix.

6 Calculate the breakeven sales.

Example

1 $(£7 \times 5) + (£15 \times 1) = £50$

2 $(£4 \times 5) + (£10 \times 1) = £30$

3 $(£30 \div £50) \times 100\% = 60\%$

4 Fixed costs $\div$ C/S ratio = £30,000 $\div$ 0.6
= £50,000

5 $(£7 \times 5) : (£15 \times 1) = 35 : 15$ or $7 : 3$

6 M = £50,000 $\times$ 7/10 = £35,000
N = £50,000 $\times$ 3/10 = £15,000
£50,000

Calculation of breakeven sales: approach 2

You may just be provided with individual C/S ratios.

Example

C/S ratio of X = 45%

C/S ratio of Y = 35%

Ratio of sales = 3:4

$$\text{Average C/S ratio} = \frac{(45\% \times 3) + (35\% \times 4)}{7}$$

$$= 39.3\%$$

You can then carry on from step **4** as earlier.

Target contributions

Example (J Co)

J Co wishes to earn contribution of £500,000.

Sales revenue = (£1 ÷ C/S ratio) × £500,000
= (£1 ÷ 0.6*) × £500,000 = £833,333

* from example on page 24

Any change in the proportions of products in the mix will change the contribution per mix and the average C/S ratio and hence the breakeven point.

Most profitable mix option

Suppose J Co (from our example) has the option of changing the sales ratio to 2M to 4N. Which is the optimal mix?

1 Calculate breakeven point in number of mixes.

2 Calculate breakeven point in units and revenue.

Example (J Co)

1 Mix 1: 1,000 mixes (calculated earlier)

Mix 2: Contribution per mix = (£4 × 2) + (£10 × 4)
= £48

Breakeven point = £30,000 ÷ £48
= 625 mixes

2 Mix 1: £50,000 (calculated earlier)

Mix 2: M   625 × 2   = 1,250 units
1,250 × £7 = £8,750 units

N   625 × 4   = 2,500 units
2,500 × £15 = £37,500 revenue

Total breakeven revenue = £46,250

Mix 2 is preferable because it requires a lower level of sales to break even (because it has a higher average contribution per unit sold of £48/6 = £8 (compared with £30/6 = £5 for mix 1).

Changing the product mix

ABC Co sells products Alpha and Beta in the ratio 5:1 at the same selling price per unit. Beta has a C/S ratio of 66.67% and the overall C/S ratio is 58.72%. How do we calculate the overall C/S ratio if the mix is changed to 2:5?

1 Calculate the missing C/S ratio

- Calculate original market share (Alpha 5/6, Beta 1/6).
- Calculate weighted C/S ratios.

  Beta: $0.6667 \times 0.1667 = 0.1111$
  Alpha: $0.5872 - 0.1111 = 0.4761$

- Calculate the missing C/S ratio.

	Alpha	Beta	Total
C/S ratio	0.5713 *	0.6667	
Market share	× 0.8333	× 0.1667	
	0.4761	0.1111	0.5872

* 0.4761/0.8333

2 Calculate the revised overall C/S ratio

	Alpha	Beta	Total
C/S ratio (as in 1)	0.5713	0.6667	
Market share (2/7:5/7)	× 0.2857	× 0.7143	
	0.1632	0.4762	0.6394

The overall C/S ratio has increased because of the increase in the proportion of the mix of the Beta, which has the higher C/S ratio.

Target profits: approach 1

1 Calculate the contribution per mix.

2 Calculate the required number of mixes.

3 Calculate the required number of units and sales revenue of each product.

You should remember from your earlier studies that the contribution required to earn a target profit (P) = fixed costs + P.

Example (J Co)

Suppose J Co wishes to earn profit of £24,900.

1 £30 (as earlier)

2 (Fixed costs + required profit)/contribution per mix = £(30,000 + 24,900)/£30 = 1,830 mixes

	£
3 M: (1,830 × 5) units for (× £7)	64,050
N: (1,830 × 1) units for (× £15)	27,450
Total revenue	91,500
Variable costs (9,150 × £3) + (1,830 × £5)	36,600
Fixed costs	30,000
Profit	24,900

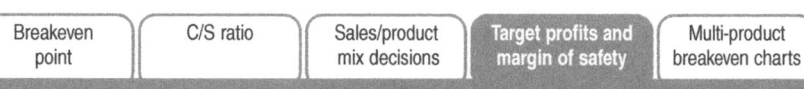

Target profits: approach 2

1 Calculate the average C/S ratio.

2 Calculate the required total revenue.

Example (J Co)

1 60% (from earlier)

2 Required contribution ÷ C/S ratio
= (fixed costs + profit) ÷ C/S ratio
= £54,900 ÷ 0.6 = £91,500

Margin of safety

1 Calculate the breakeven point in revenue.

2 Calculate the margin of safety.

Example (J Co)

Suppose J Co has budgeted sales of £62,000.

1 £50,000 (from earlier)

2 Budgeted sales – breakeven sales
= £(62,000 – 50,000) = £12,000
= 19.4% of budgeted sales

Breakeven chart

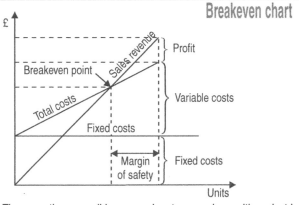

A multi-product breakeven chart can only be drawn on the assumption that the sales proportions are fixed.

There are three possible approaches to preparing multi-product breakeven charts.

1 Output in £ sales and a constant product mix

2 Products in sequence

3 Output in tems of % of forecast sales and a constant product mix

P/V chart

Suppose J's sales budget is 6,000 units of M and 1,200 units of N.

Revenue (6,000 × £7 + 1,200 × £15) = £60,000

Variable costs (6,000 × £3 + 1,200 × £5) = £24,000

On the chart, products are shown individually, from left to right, in order of size of decreasing C/S ratio.

	C/S ratio	Cum sales £'000	Cum profit £'000
N	66.67%	18	*(18)
M	57.14%	60	6

* (1,200 × £15) – (12,000 × £5) – £30,000

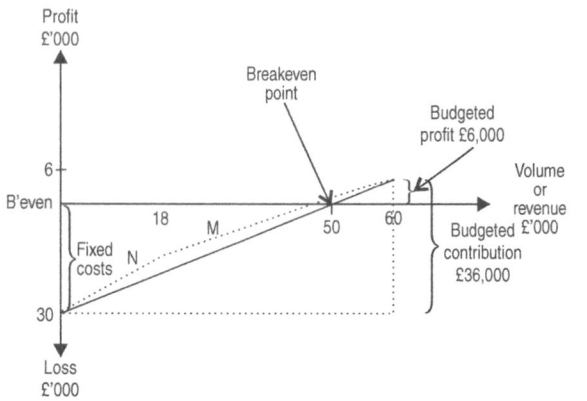

What the multi-product P/V chart highlights

- The overall company breakeven point

- Which products should be expanded in output (the most profitable in terms of C/S ratio) and which, if any, should be discontinued

- What effect changes in selling price and sales revenue would have on breakeven point and profit

- The average profit (the solid line which joins the two ends of the dotted line) earned from the sales of the products in the mix

Notes

8: Short-term decision-making

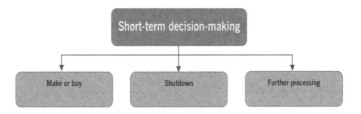

Decision-making scenarios	Make or buy decisions	Either/or problems	Shutdown problems	Allocation of joint costs

Acceptance/rejection of contracts

If an organisation does not have spare capacity, existing business should only be turned away if the contribution from a contract is greater than the contribution from the business which must be sacrificed.

Extra shift decisions and overtime

The decision to work an extra shift should be taken on the basis of whether the costs of the shift are exceeded by the benefits to be obtained.

Minimum pricing

The minimum price for a one-off product or service contract is its total relevant cost. This is the price at which the company would make no incremental profit or loss from undertaking the work, but would just achieve an incremental cost breakeven point.

Key points

- Number workings consecutively.
- Label tables and workings with headings and show units (£, kgs, etc).
- On a separate page, do a summary and state your conclusion.
- Cross reference your summary to your workings.

No scarce resources

The relevant costs of the decision are the differential costs between making and buying.

Further considerations

- How to use freed up capacity
- Could using an outside supplier cause an industrial dispute?
- Subcontractor reliability with delivery and product quality
- Loss of flexibility and control by subcontracting

With scarce resources

If an organisation has to subcontract because of insufficient in-house resources, total costs are minimised if those units bought have the lowest extra variable cost of buying (compared with making in-house) per unit of scarce resource saved by buying.

Example (limited labour time)

	A	B
Variable cost of making	£16	£14
Variable cost of buying	£20	£19
Extra variable cost of buying	£4	£5
Labour hours saved by buying	2	2
Extra variable cost of buying per hour saved	£2	£2.50
Priority for making in-house	2nd	1st

The best approach is to draw up a three-column table with columns for the first option, for the second option and for the differences between the options.

- Do savings and costs separately and put one type in brackets. It doesn't matter which way round you do this as long as you are consistent within the question.

- Subtract column 2 from column 1, taking care with minus signs: −50,000 −(−45,000) = −5,000

Example

		Option 1 £	Option 2 £	Net (savings)/ costs £	
Savings	Saving 1	(500)	(100)	(400)	**Conclusion.** Option 1 costs £400 more than option 2. (Alternatively, option 2 would bring savings of £400 more than option 1.)
	Saving 2	(300)	(600)	300	
Costs	Cost 1	0	200	(200)	
	Cost 2	700	0	700	
Net cost				400	

Shutdown problems involve decisions about whether to close down a product line, department or other activity, perhaps because it is making losses or running costs are too expensive and if the decision is to shut down, whether the closure should be permanent or temporary.

Other (non-quantifiable) considerations

In practice this sort of decision has long-term consequences.

- Is the closure to be a permanent reduction in capacity, and is this desirable?
- What is the impact on employees, customers, competitors and suppliers?

Financial considerations

The basic method is to use short-run relevant costs to calculate contributions and profits or losses.

1. Calculate what is earned by the process at present (perhaps in comparison with others).

2. Calculate what will be the financial consequences of closing down (selling machines, redundancy costs etc).

3. Compare the results and act accordingly.

4. Bear in mind that some fixed costs may no longer be incurred if the decision is to shut down and they are therefore relevant to the decision.

Joint products

Two or more products produced by the same process and separated in processing, each having a sufficiently high saleable value to merit recognition as a main product

Distinguishing features of joint products

- They are produced in the same process.
- They are indistinguishable from each other until the separation point.
- They each have a substantial sales value (after further processing, if necessary).
- They may require future processing after the separation point.

Apportioning joint costs

Costs incurred up to the point of separation (**split-off point**) need to be apportioned between the joint products for the purposes of inventory valuation, profitability analysis and pricing.

Joint product costs are not used for decision making.

There are four methods of doing this.

1 Physical measurement

- Cost is apportioned on the basis of the proportion that the output of each product bears by weight or volume to the total output.

- It is unsuitable where products separate during processing into different states.

- It ignores sales value and may lead to inappropriate results if sales values and volumes differ significantly.

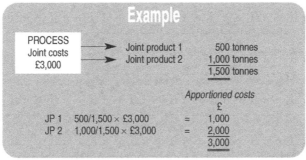

2 Sales value at split-off point

Cost is apportioned according to product's ability to produce income (that is, in the proportions that the sales value of the products bear to the sales value of the process's total output).

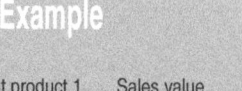

Example

PROCESS			£
Joint costs £3,000	Joint product 1	Sales value	5,000
	Joint product 2	Sales value	10,000
			15,000

	£
JP 1 apportioned costs = 5,000/15,000 × £3,000 =	1,000
JP 2 apportioned costs = 10,000/15,000 × £3,000 =	2,000
	3,000

3 Sales value minus further processing costs

If the sales value at split-off point is not available, costs can be apportioned on the basis of residual/notional/proxy sales value (final sales value minus further processing costs).

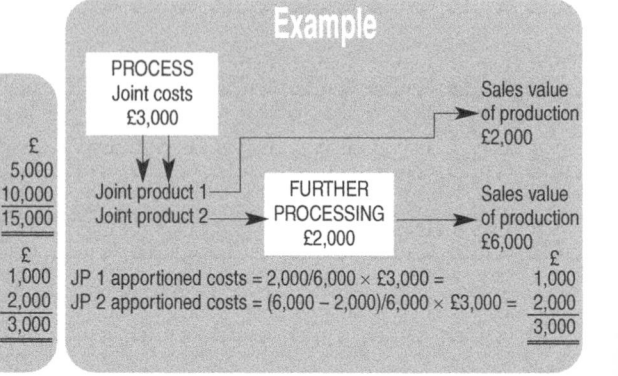

Example

PROCESS		Sales value
Joint costs £3,000		of production £2,000
Joint product 1	FURTHER	Sales value
Joint product 2	PROCESSING £2,000	of production £6,000

	£
JP 1 apportioned costs = 2,000/6,000 × £3,000 =	1,000
JP 2 apportioned costs = (6,000 – 2,000)/6,000 × £3,000 =	2,000
	3,000

4 Weighted average method

If 'units' of joint product are not comparable in terms of physical resemblance or physical weight (gas, liquid, solid etc), joint costs are apportioned on the basis of 'weighted units' (units of joint product × weighting factor).

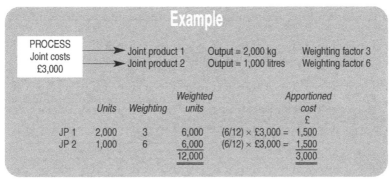

Further processing decision

A product should be further processed if its sales revenue minus its further processing costs exceeds its sales revenue at the split-off point. The apportionment of joint processing costs is irrelevant to the decision.

By-products

A supplementary or secondary product (arising as the result of a process), the value of which is small relative to that of the principal product(s).

Possible accounting treatments of by-products

- Add the net sales revenue from the by-product to sales revenue of the main product.

- Treat the sales revenue of the by-product as a separate incidental source of revenue ('other income').

- Deduct the sales revenue of the by-product from the cost of production/sales of the main product.

- Deduct the net realisable value of the by-product from the cost of production of the main product (most common method).

Do NOT allocate joint costs to a by-product.

9: Linear programming: the graphical method

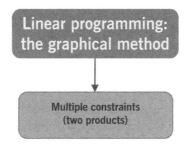

Linear programming

A technique for allocating scarce resources so as to maximise or minimise a range of numerical quantities (although most commonly to maximise contribution or minimise costs)

Which technique to use		
Number of products	**Number of scarce resources**	**Technique**
Any number	1	Limiting factor analysis
2	Any number	Graphical approach to linear programming
3 or more	Any number	Simplex approach to linear programming (not on your syllabus)

This example will be used throughout the chapter.

Example

A company makes two products with relevant data as follows.

	Standard	Deluxe	Availability per month
Contribution per unit	£15	£20	
Labour hours per unit	5	10	4,000
Kgs of material per unit	10	5	4,250

Find the production plan which will maximise contribution.

1 Define variables

- Let x = number of Standard produced each month
- Let y = number of Deluxe produced each month

2 Establish objective function

Maximise contribution (C) = 15x + 20y subject to the following constraints

3 Establish constraints

- Labour: $5x + 10y \leq 4,000$
- Material: $10x + 5y \leq 4,250$
- Non negativity: $x \geq 0, y \geq 0$

Feasible region

The area within all the constraint lines in a linear programming graph, which contains all feasible combinations of output.

Students often have problems with constraints of the style 'the quantity of one type must not exceed twice that of the other'. This can be interpreted as follows: the quantity of one type (say X) must not exceed (must be less than or equal to) twice that of the other (2Y) (ie X ≤ 2Y).

4 Graph the problem

- Labour: $5x + 10y = 4{,}000$; if $x = 0$, $y = 400$, and if $y = 0$, $x = 800$

- Material: $10x + 5y = 4{,}250$; if $x = 0$, $y = 850$, and if $y = 0$, $x = 425$

5 Define feasible area/region

This is the area where *all* inequalities are satisfied (area above x axis and y axis ($x \geq 0$, $y \geq 0$), below material constraint ($\leq$) *and* below labour constraint ($\leq$)).

If you have to draw a graph make sure that it has a title, that the axes are labelled and that the constraint lines and feasible area are clearly identified.

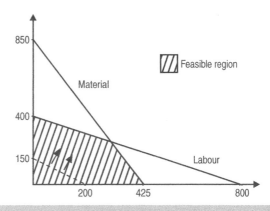

6 Determine optimal solution

Method 1

- Add an **iso-contribution line** (suppose C = £3,000 so that if C = 15x + 20y, then if x = 0, y = 150, and if y = 0, x = 200).

- (Sliding your ruler across the page if necessary) find the point furthest from the origin but still in the feasible area.

- Use simultaneous equations to find out the x and y coordinates at the optimal solution, the intersection of the material and labour constraints (x = 300, y = 250)(or find them directly from the graph).

Method 2

- Determine all possible intersection points of constraints and axes using simultaneous equations.

- Calculate contribution at each intersection point to determine which is the optimal solution.

> If the iso-contribution line is exactly parallel to one of the constraint lines there will not be a single optimum solution, but a range of solutions along the part of the line within the feasible area.

Whatever the objective of the linear programming problem, the optimal solution is the one that yields the largest value for the objective function in the case of a maximisation problem, the lowest value in the case of a minimisation problem.

Minimisation problems

If the objective were to minimise costs the optimal solution would be at the point in the feasible area closest to the origin.

Slack and surplus

If a resource which has a maximum availability is not binding at the optimal solution, there will be slack.

If a minimum quantity of a resource must be used and, in the optimal solution, more than this quantity is used, there is a surplus on the minimum requirement.

Shadow price

> The extra contribution or profit that may be earned by relaxing by one unit a binding resource constraint

- Calculated on the basis that the extra available resource costs the normal variable amount.
- Represent the maximum premium above the normal variable amount that an organisation should be willing to pay for one extra unit of a resource.
- Since shadow prices indicate the effect of a one unit change in a constraint, they provide a measure of the sensitivity of a result.
- The shadow price of a constraint that is not binding at the optimal solution is zero.
- Only valid for a small range before the constraint becomes non-binding or different resources become critical.
- Enable management to make better informed decisions about payment of overtime premium, bonuses, premiums on small orders of raw materials etc.

Example

Suppose the sales price of the Standard in our earlier example is reduced by £6 so that contribution becomes £9.

Now C = 9x + 20y

An iso-contribution line would now have a shallower slope parallel to, say, 9x + 20y = 1,800.

This iso-contribution line would leave the feasible area at the intersection of the labour constraint and the y axis (0, 400).

If x's selling price reduces by £6, the optimal solution is to produce 400 units of y, but no units of x.

Limiting factor sensitivity analysis

Example

Suppose the availability of labour was reduced by one hour.

The optimal solution would be at the intersection of $5x + 10y = 3,999$ and $10x + 5y = 4,250$.

Solution by simultaneous equations now gives $x = 300.067$ units, $y = 249.867$ units.

	£
Profit with original constraints $((15 \times 300) + (20 \times 250))$	9,500
Revised profit $((15 \times 300.067) + (20 \times 249.867))$	9,498
Reduction in contribution from loss of one labour hour	2

Shadow price of one hour of labour = £2

Profit would increase by £2 if an additional labour hour was made available (assuming the additional labour cost the normal variable cost) as long as labour is a limiting factor.

Labour would cease to be a limiting factor when the labour constraint passes through the intersection of the material constraint and the y axis $(0, 850)$ ie when availability $(5x + 10y) = (5 \times 0) + (10 \times 850)$

$= 8,500$ hours.

Further assumptions (in addition to those which apply to limiting factor analysis)

- The total amount of each scare resource is known with certainty.
- There is no interdependence between the demand for different products.

Uses

- Selling different products
- Calculation of relevant costs
- Maximum payment for additional scarce resources
- Budgeting
- Control
- Capital budgeting

Practical difficulties

- The identification of resources in short supply and their availability is problematic.
- Management may opt for a 'satisfactory' product mix rather than one that is profit maximising.
- The assumption of linearity may be totally invalid. For example the learning effect may be relevant.
- The model is essential static.
- Variables can only take on integer values.
- The shadow price only applies up to a certain limit.

Notes

10: Forecasting techniques

Linear regression analysis (least squares technique) finds the equation of the straight line **(line of best fit)** which has the general form **Y = a +bX**

where **Y = dependent variable = total cost**
  X = independent variable = level of activity
  a = intercept of line on y axis = fixed cost
  b = gradient of line = variable cost per unit

Historical data (adjusted for inflation) provide readings for x and y. These readings are then substituted into formulae for a and b.

$$b = \frac{n\Sigma XY - \Sigma X\Sigma Y}{n\Sigma X^2 - (\Sigma X)^2} \text{ and } a = \frac{\Sigma Y}{n} - \frac{b\Sigma X}{n}$$

where n = number of pairs of data for X and Y.

> The formulae for a and b will be provided in the exam.

Conditions necessary for the use of linear regression analysis

- A linear cost function is assumed.
- Historical cost data is accurately recorded.
- There are 10+ pairs of data.
- The activity levels in the historical data cover the full normal range of activity.
- Data is adjusted to account for inflation.
- Past conditions are indicative of future conditions.
- The value of Y can be predicted from the value of X.

Regression analysis and forecasting

Forecasting costs

Once the equation has been determined, a value for X (activity level) can be substituted into the equation and a value for Y (total cost at that activity level) forecast.

Example

Calculations produce $Y = 17 + 3.6X$ (where X is in '000 units and Y is in £'000). Fixed costs are therefore £17,000 and variable cost per unit is £3,600.

Predicted cost (Y) if activity level (X) is 13,000 units = $17 + (3.6 \times 13) = 63.8 = £63,800$

Forecasting sales

1. Calculate a regression line (trend line) $Y = a + bX$, where Y = sales and X = period of time.

2. Years (days/months) become the X variable in the regression formulae by numbering them from 1 upwards.

3. A forecast (Y) for a particular time period (X) is determined by substitution of the value for X into the trend line equation.

Example

Year	X	Sales (Y) '000 units
20X0	1	21
20X1	2	23	extract
20X2	3	26

Calculations produce $Y = 18 + 2.7X$

Predicted sales (Y) in 20X6 (X = 7)
$$= 18 + (2.7 \times 7)$$
$$= 36.9$$
$$= £36,900 \text{ units}$$

Correlation

The extent to which the value of a dependent variable is related to the value of an independent variable

Coefficient of correlation, r

Also known as the **Pearsonian coefficient of correlation** or the **product moment correlation coefficient**, this measures the degree of correlation.

$$r = \frac{n\sum XY - \sum X \sum Y}{\sqrt{(n\sum X^2 - (\sum X)^2)(n\sum Y^2 - (\sum Y)^2)}}$$

r has a value between –1 (perfect negative correlation) and +1 (perfect positive correlation)

Degrees of correlation

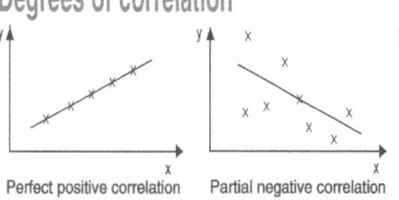

Perfect positive correlation   Partial negative correlation   No correlation

Perfect negative correlation and partial positive correlation are also possible.

Coefficient of determination, r²

This indicates the change in Y that can be predicted by a change in X.

If $r^2 = 0.95$, 95% of the variation in the value of Y can be predicted from variations in X.

The closer r^2 is to 1, the greater the degree of confidence that X (level of activity) can be used to accurately predict Y (cost).

Finding the trend (T)

1. The trend line can be drawn **by eye** on a graph as a line of best fit.

2. **Linear regression analysis** (see page 100)

3. **Moving averages**

Of an even number of periods

Year	Sales	Moving total of 4 yrs' sales	Moving average of 4 yrs' sales	Mid-point of 2 moving av'ges TREND
20X1	600			
20X2	840			
		2,580*	645.0	
20X3	420			650.00
		2,620**	655.0	
20X4	720			
20X5	640			

*(600+840+420+720)   **(840+420+720+640)

Of an odd number of periods

Year	Sales	Moving total of 3 yrs' sales	Moving av. of 3 yrs' sales (÷3) TREND
20X0	390		
20X1	380	1,230	410
20X2	460	1,290	430
20X3	450		

Finding the seasonal variations (SV)

1 **Calculate the seasonal variations**

- **Additive model** $(TS = T + SV + R)$

  Assuming R is relatively small:

  $SV = \text{actual} - \text{trend} \ (SV = TS - T)$

- **Multiplicative model**

  $(TS = T \times SV \times R)$ Assuming R is small:

  $SV = \text{actual} \div \text{trend} \ (SV = TS/T)$

2 **Take an average of the variations**

			Seasonal variation	
Wk 1	Actual	Trend	Add model	Multi model
M	80	92.70	−12.70	0.863
T	104	93.12	+10.88	1.117

	Additive model		Multiplicative model	
	M	T	M	T
Wk 1	−12.70	+10.88	0.863	1.117
Wk 2	−12.80	+14.78	0.865	1.155
Total	−25.50	+25.66	1.728	2.272
Average	−12.75	+12.83	0.864	1.136

3 **Adjust the total of the variations**

Additive model: to zero

	Mon	Tues	Wed	Thurs	Fri	Total
Average	−12.75	+12.83	+0.91	+27.49	−32.43	−3.95
Adjustment (3.95/5)	+0.79	+0.79	+0.79	+0.79	+0.79	+3.95
Final estimate	−11.96	13.62	1.70	28.28	−31.64	0.00
Round to	−12	14	2	28	−32	

Multiplicative model: to number of items in cycle

	Mon	Tues	Wed	Thurs	Fri	Total
Average	0.8640	1.1360	1.0095	1.2890	0.6600	4.9585
Adjustment (5 − 4.9585)/5	0.0083	0.0083	0.0083	0.0083	0.0083	0.0415
Final estimate	0.8723	1.1443	1.0178	1.2973	0.6683	5.0000
Round to	0.87	1.14	1.02	1.3	0.67	

Time series analysis and forecasting

Calculate a trend line and then use the trend line to forecast future values and adjust these values by the applicable seasonal variation.

- **Using inspection** (extend the line of best fit)
- **Linear regression analysis** (the sales forecast (Y) for a particular time period (X) is determined by substituting the value for X into the trend line equation)
- **Common sense**

Example

1

| Year | Trend values (quarter) | | | |
	1st	2nd	3rd	4th
1			18.75	19.375
2	20	20.5	21	21.5
3	22.125	22.75		

2 Average seasonal variations for quarters 1 to 4 are –0.1, +12.4, +1.1 and –13.4 respectively.

3 The trend line indicates an increase of about 0.6 per quarter, which can be checked as follows.

$$\frac{22.75\,(Yr3Q_2) - 18.75\,(Yr1Q_3)}{7\,(\text{Number of Qs})} = 0.57 \approx 0.6$$

4 Trend line forecast for year 4 quarter 1 is as follows.

YearQ						Trend line
3	2nd	actual trend	22.75, say			22.8
	3rd	forecast trend	= 22.8 + 0.6	=		23.4
	4th	forecast trend	= 23.4 + 0.6	=		24.0
4	1st	forecast trend	= 24.0 + 0.6	=		24.6

5 Final forecast = 24.6 – 0.1 (seasonal variation) = 24.5

6 If the multiplicative model variation for quarter 1 was 0.98, year 4 quarter 1 prediction = 24.6 × 0.98 = 24.1

Forecasting with scatter diagrams

1. Plot cost and activity data on a graph.
2. Draw a 'line of best fit' through the middle of the plotted points.
3. Fixed costs = intercept on vertical axis
4. Variable cost per unit = (total cost (read from the graph) – fixed cost) ÷ activity level

Forecasting problems

- Political, economic, environmental, technological and social changes make forecasting difficult.
- The further into the future the forecast, the more unreliable it is.
- The less data available for the forecast, the less reliable it is.
- The pattern of trend and seasonal variations may not continue.

Factors to consider when forecasting sales

- Past sales patterns
- New technology
- Market research results
- Changing consumer tastes
- Legislation
- Economic environment
- Anticipated advertising
- Pricing policies and discounts offered
- Environment
- Competition
- Available mathematical techniques

Notes

11a: Budgets for planning

Objectives of a budgetary planning and control system

- P – Planning (compel planning)
- R – Responsibility
- I – Integration and co-ordination
- M – Motivation
- E – Evaluation and control

You need to be able to explain why organisations prepare plans. Planning forces management to look ahead, to set out detailed plans for achieving the targets for each department, operation and (ideally) each manager, and to anticipate problems. It therefore prevents managers from relying on ad hoc or uncoordinated planning which may be detrimental to the performance of the organisation.

Planning

The overall planning process covers both the long term and the short term.

Types of planning

- **Strategic/corporate/long-range planning** (selecting strategies to attain objectives)
- **Budgetary/short-term tactical planning** (preparing detailed plans covering one year)
- **Operation planning** (planning on a day-to-day basis how resources will be used)

1 Communication of objectives

2 Identification of the principal budget factor

3 Preparation of functional budgets (eg sales, production, labour, materials)

4 Co-ordination of budget

5 Preparation of master budget (budgeted income statement, budgeted statement of financial position, cash budget)

6 Ongoing review of budgets

Standard hours

If you are asked to prepare the labour budget for the production of a number of dissimilar units, you can convert the budgeted output into standard hours of production and construct a labour budget accordingly.

You must be able to recommend action given the information shown in budgets prepared.

Examples of appropriate action

If a budget indicates a shortfall in labour hours, you could suggest overtime working, reduction in wastage, or improvement in productivity.

If a budget indicates that capacity will exceed sales demand for a length of time, consideration should be given to product diversification, a reduction in selling price (if demand is elastic) and so on. A shortfall in capacity might require overtime, subcontracting, machine hire or new sources of materials.

Steps in the preparation of a cash budget

1   Set up a proforma.

2   Establish budgeted sales month by month. Bearing in mind the credit period taken by trade receivables and taking discounts into account, calculate when budgeted sales revenue will be received as cash and when opening receivables will pay.

3   Establish when any other cash income will be received.

4   Establish, for each month, production quantities and hence materials usage quantities, materials inventory changes and the quantity and cost of materials purchases. Bearing in mind the credit period taken, calculate when cash payments to suppliers will be made and when the amount due to opening payables will be paid.

5   Establish when any other cash payments (excluding non-cash items such as depreciation) will be paid.

> Include at the foot of every column of your cash budget the opening cash position, the net cash flow and the closing cash position.

Usefulness

The cash budget shows the cash position as a result of all plans made during the budgetary process and so gives management the opportunity to take appropriate control action.

Appropriate control action

- **Short-term surplus.** Pay payables (creditors) early to obtain discount or make short-term investments
- **Short-term deficit.** Increase payables, reduce receivables, arrange an overdraft
- **Long-term surplus.** Expand, diversify, replace/update non-current assets
- **Long-term deficit.** Issue share capital, consider shutdown/divestment opportunities

Cash flow versus profit

These are likely to be different.

- Not all cash receipts affect income statement income (eg issue of new shares)
- Not all cash payments affect income statement expenditure (eg purchase of non-current assets)
- Some items in the income statement are not cash flows (eg depreciation)
- Timings of cash receipts and payments may not coincide with income statement recording (eg declaration and payment of dividend)

Bad debts will never be recovered in cash and doubtful debts may not be received, so adjust if necessary for such items.

Incremental budgeting

This involves adding a certain percentage to last year's budget to allow for growth and inflation. It encourages slack and wasteful spending to creep into budgets.

contrast with

Zero-based budgeting (ZBB)

This approach treats the preparation of the budget for each period as an independent planning exercise: the initial budget is zero and every item of expenditure has to be justified in its entirety to be included.

Three-step approach to ZBB

1 Define **decision packages** (description of a specific activity so that it can be evaluated and ranked).

Mutually exclusive packages ← → **Incremental packages**

2 Evaluate and rank packages on the basis of their benefit to the organisation.

3 Allocate resources according to the funds available and the ranking of packages.

Advantages of ZBB

☑ Identifies and removes inefficient and/or obsolete operations

☑ Forces employees to avoid wasteful expenditure

☑ Leads to a more efficient allocation of resources

☑ Challenges the status quo

Disadvantages of ZBB

☒ Involves time and effort

☒ Can cause suspicion when introduced

☒ Costs and benefits of different alternative courses of action can be difficult to quantify

☒ Ranking can prove problematic

☒ Short term v long term trade-off

Applications of ZBB

- Support expenses
- Service industries
- Not-for-profit organisations
- Discretionary costs
- Rationalisation measures

Programme planning and budgeting systems (PPBS)

PPBS set a budget in terms of programmes (groups of activities with common objectives). By focusing on objectives, the budget is orientated towards the ultimate output of the organisation (which contrasts with the traditional approach to budgeting, which focuses on inputs (labour, material, etc)).

Particular uses of PPBS

- Public sector
- Non-profit seeking organisations

PPBS ensures expenditure is focused on the programmes/ activities that generate the most beneficial results and is in line with public demands for **accountability**.

Disadvantages of traditional budgeting for non-profit seeking organisations

- Activities span several years, but the emphasis is on annual figures.
- It is difficult to incorporate the mainly non-financial planned/actual achievements.
- Costs for a particular objective are spread across a number of cost categories.
- There is no evidence of how effectively/efficiently resources are used.

Discretionary costs

Costs of a process for which there is no clear relationship between its input and its output, often because the output is difficult to measure, in terms of quantity and/or quality

Budgeting for discretionary costs

This can be made easier by converting them into engineered costs.

- Develop suitable output measures
- Understand how input impacts on output

ABC might be useful.

If a discretionary cost cannot be converted into an engineered cost, ZBB or PPBS will be needed.

It is obviously much easier to budget for direct material cost (an engineered cost) than for the cost of the accounts department (discretionary cost).

Control of discretionary costs

Control (perhaps minimum standards of performance) is problematic because some measure of output is required. Inputs can be controlled, however, if the budget acts as a device to ensure financial resources allocated to the activity are not exceeded.

11b: Budgets for performance evaluation

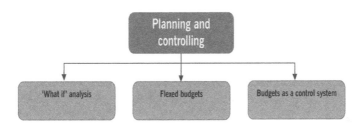

Fixed budgets

These are prepared on the basis of an estimated volume of production and an estimated volume of sales. No variants of the budget are made to cover the event that actual and budgeted activity levels differ and they are not adjusted (in retrospect) to reflect actual activity levels.

Budgetary control

This is the practice of establishing budgets which identify areas of responsibility for individual managers and of regularly comparing actual results against expected results (using a flexible budget). The resulting variances provide guidelines for management control action.

Flexible budgets

These are budgets which, by recognising different cost behaviour patterns, change as activity levels change.

- At the planning stage, flexible budgets can be drawn up to show the effect of the actual volumes of output and sales differing from budgeted volumes.

- At the end of a period, actual results can be compared to a flexed budget (*what results should have been at actual output and sales volumes*) as a control procedure.

Example

Suppose that J Co has prepared budgeted profit forecasts based on 90%, 100% (50,000 units) and 105% activity.

	Budgets			
	90%	100%	105%	Actual (37,500 units sold)
	$	$	$	$
Revenue	1,350,000	1,500,000	1,575,000	1,075,000
Costs				
Materials	337,500	375,000	393,750	311,750
Labour	405,000	450,000	472,500	351,500
Production overhead	120,000	130,000	135,000	117,500
Admin overhead	70,000	70,000	70,000	66,500
	932,500	1,025,000	1,071,250	847,250
Profit	417,500	475,000	503,750	227,750

1. Decide whether costs are fixed, variable or semi-variable.

2. Split semi-variable costs into their fixed and variable components using the high-low method.

3. Flex the budget to the required activity level.

A budgetary control report for J Co is shown below.

	Flexed budget	Actual	Variance
	$	$	$
Revenue	1,125,000 (W1)	1,075,000	50,000 (A)
Costs			
Materials	281,250 (W2)	311,750	30,500 (A)
Labour	337,500 (W3)	351,500	14,000 (A)
Prod o/h	105,000 (W4)	117,500	12,500 (A)
Admin o/h	70,000 (W5)	66,500	3,500 (F)
	793,750	847,250	53,500 (A)
Profit	331,250	227,750	103,500 (A)

Workings

1 $37,500 \times (1,500,000/50,000)$

2 Material costs are variable.
   Costs per unit = $\$375,000/50,000 = \$7.50$
   Budget cost allowance = $\$7.50 \times 37,500$

3 Labour costs are variable.
   Cost per unit = $\$450,000/50,000 = \$9$
   Budget cost allowance = $\$9 \times 37,500$

4 Production overhead is a semi-variable cost
   At 90%, activity level = $50,000 \times 0.9 = 45,000$ units.
   Variable cost of $(50,000 - 45,000)$ units = $\$(130,000 - 120,000)$.
   $\therefore$ Variable cost per unit = $\$10,000/5,000 = \$2$.
   $\therefore$ Fixed cost = $\$(130,000 - (50,000 \times \$2)) = \$30,000$
   Budget cost allowance = $\$(30,000 + (37,500 \times \$2))$

5 Administration overhead is a fixed cost.

How can computers help with budgetary control?

- Calculation of flexed budget
- Detailed variance analysis
- Speedy production of control information

Budgetary control reports

Budget holders must receive these regularly so they can monitor the budget centre's operations and take necessary control action.

11b: Budgets for performance evaluation

Managers of responsibility centres should only be held accountable for costs over which they have some influence. A distinction is therefore made between controllable and uncontrollable costs.

- **Most variable costs** are controllable in the short term.

- Some **fixed costs** are discretionary but most are uncontrollable in the short term.

- **Directly attributable fixed costs** are fixed in the short term within the relevant range but a drastic reduction in a department's output, say, would reduce/remove them.

- A cost **uncontrollable by a junior manager** might be **controllable by a senior manager** (eg overtime).

- A cost **uncontrollable by a manger in one department** may be **controllable by a manager in another** (see example).

Example

An increase in material costs might be caused by buying at higher prices than expected (controllable by the purchasing department) or by excessive wastage/spoilage (controllable by the production department).

Feedback
Two meanings

The **process** of reporting back control information to management ←→ The **control information** itself (produced from within the organisation to help management/ employees with control decisions)

Single loop feedback

- Feedback of relatively small variations between actual and plan so that corrective action can bring performance in line with planned results

- Existing plans will not change

Double-loop (higher-level) feedback

- Ensures plans are revised to meet changes in conditions

−
- Targets were missed
- Control action needed

+
- Targets hit were better than those aimed at
- Move the target

Features of feedback information

- Clear and comprehensive
- 'Exception principle' applied
- Identifies controllable costs

- Timely
- Accurate
- Communicated to correct manager

11b: Budgets for performance evaluation

Feedforward control

Control based on comparing original targets or actual results with a forecast of future results

1 Compare the **current forecast with the plan** to ascertain whether control action must be taken to get back to the plan.

2 Prepare a **revised forecast** to account for the effects of control action.

3 Compare the **revised forecast with the plan** to determine whether the plan will be achieved.

4 Compare the **original forecast with the revised forecast** to show the expected effect of control action.

5 At the end of the control period

- Compare **actual results with the revised forecast** (why did differences occur?)
- Compare **actual results with the plan** (how close are actual results to the plan?)

6 Prepare a **new forecast** and begin the control cycle again.

12a: Standard costing

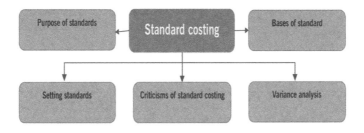

Although it can be used in a variety of costing situations, the greatest benefit from standard costing can be gained if there is a degree of repetition in the production process (mass production and repetitive assembly work).

Note that a standard cost per task can be calculated if there is a similarity of tasks. In this way standard costing can be used by some service organisations.

Uses of standard costing

- To act as a control device (variance analysis)
- To value inventory and cost production
- To assist in setting budgets and evaluating managerial performance
- To enable the principle of 'management by exception' to be practised
- To provide a prediction of future costs for use in decision-making situations
- To motivate staff and management by providing challenging targets
- To provide guidance on possible ways of improving efficiency

Allowing for inflation in material and labour cost standards

- Use of current price as standard produces constantly increasing adverse variances.
- Use of an estimated mid-year price produces favourable variances in the first half of the year, adverse variances in the second half.

Evolution and continuous improvement

- A standard needs to evolve over a few accounting periods before it can be used as a useful measure for control purposes.
- Standards can be continuously improved by refined/increased standard-setting procedures or revision of standards.

Types of performance standard

Ideal
- Perfect operating conditions
- Unfavourable motivational impact

Attainable
- Allowances made for inefficiencies and wastage
- Incentive to work harder (realistic but challenging)

Current
- Based on current working conditions
- No motivational impact

Basic
- Unaltered over a long period of time
- Unfavourable impact on performance

Setting standards for overheads

Standard absorption rate (predetermined OAR) depends on planned **production volume**, which depends on two factors:

- **production capacity** (in standard hours of output) and **efficiency** of working.

Capacity can be **full**, **practical** or **budgeted**.

Example

A work force consists of 20 people, who each work a 35 hour week.

The standard time per unit = $2\frac{1}{2}$ hours and expected efficiency of the workforce = 125%.

Budgeted capacity = 20×35 = 700 production hrs/wk.

The work force should take 1 hour to produce 1.25 ($1 \times 125\%$) standard hours of output.

Budgeted output = $700 \times 125\%$ = 875 standard hours of output per week.

Budgeted production volume = $875 \div 2\frac{1}{2}$ = 350 units of output per week.

Standard costing in service industries can be problematic.

- Difficulty establishing measurable cost unit
- Every cost unit may be different
- Human influence element

Diagnostic related groups

They provide a system of classifying patients according to their diagnosis, age and length of stay.

McDonaldization attempts to overcome these problems.

- **Calculability** – content of every meal is identical and standardised

- **Control** – reducing the human influence eg automatic drinks dispensers

- **Efficiency** – as quickly and cheaply as possible for required quality of service

- **Predictability** – same in every outlet throughout the world

Enables principles of standard costing to be applied in the health service in order to maximise efficiency and minimise waste.

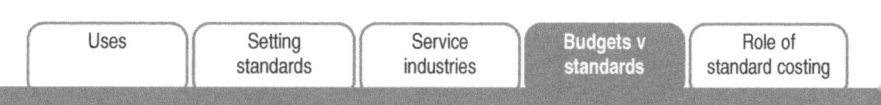

Similarities

- They both involve looking to the future and forecasting what is likely to happen given a certain set of circumstances.

- They are both used for control purposes.

Interrelationships

- A standard unit cost of production can act as the basis for a production cost budget: standard unit cost × budgeted activity level = budgeted expenditure.

Differences

- A budget gives the planned total aggregate costs for a function or cost centre whereas a standard shows unit resource usage and cost.

Criticisms of standard costing in today's environment

Standard costing has been described as unhelpful and potentially misleading in today's environment.

Standard costing	Modern environment
■ Concentrates on a narrow range of costs	■ Quality and customer satisfaction are important.
■ Too much emphasis on direct labour costs	■ Direct labour is a small proportion of costs.
■ Focuses on short-term variable costs	■ Most costs are fixed in the short term.
■ Relies on repetitive operations and homogeneous output	■ Organisations must respond to customers' changing requirements.
■ Requires stable conditions, and assumes performance to standard is acceptable	■ It is more dynamic and focused on continuous improvement.
■ Control statements produced weekly/monthly	■ Control information is required promptly.

Standard costing in a total quality environment

Standard costing environment

- Stable, standardised, repetitive environment
- Planned level of scrap
- Predetermined standards
- Concentrates on quantity
- Effectiveness = high volume of output at low cost
- Failure is measured in variances
- Labour efficiency measured in terms of individual tasks and level of output
- Labour and material variances

Total quality environment

- Continual improvement
- Zero defects
- Continual improvements alter inputs, prices etc
- Quality is the issue
- Effectiveness = high quality output from high quality input
- Failure is measured in terms of internal/external failure costs
- Efficiency of labour (responsible multi-task teams) measured in terms of reworking, returns, defects
- Minimal labour rate variances (guaranteed weekly wage) and few material price/usage variances (fixed price contracts, supplier guaranteeing quality)

Standard costing and new technology

Standard costing has traditionally been associated with labour-intensive operations. Can it be applied to capital-intensive production?

- Labour costs are a small proportion of total costs, so would labour variances have any control value?

- Fixed costs are a significant proportion of total costs but there are questions over the relevance of fixed overhead variance control information.

- Machines are more accurate than human operators so material usage variances should be non-existent.

Standard costing and JIT

Examples	
Traditionally	Avoid idle time, keep up production and so minimise adverse efficiency variances.
JIT with TQM	Such action would lead to unwanted inventory.
Traditionally	Shop around for cheapest suppliers to minimise adverse material price variances.
JIT	Focus is on supplier reliability and quality, and on establishing long-term contractual links.

Notes

12b: Basic variance analysis

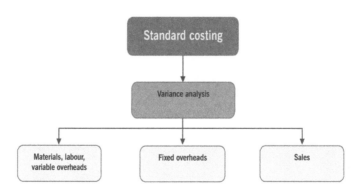

Example to be used throughout this chapter

Standard cost of product A

	£
Materials (5 kg × £10 per kg)	50
Labour (4 hrs × £5 per hour)	20
Variable o/hds (4 hrs × £2 per hour)	8
Fixed o/hds (4 hrs × £6 per hour)	24
	102

Actual results

Production	1,000 units
Sales	900 units
Materials	4,850 kg, £46,075
Labour	4,200 hrs, £21,210
Variable o/hds	£9,450
Fixed o/hds	£25,000
Selling price	£140 per unit

Budgeted results

Production	1,200 units
Sales	1,000 units
Selling price	£150 per unit

Direct material total variance

> The difference between what the output should have cost, and what it actually cost, in terms of material

This can be divided into two sub-variances.

Direct material price variance

> The difference between what the material used should have cost and what it did cost

Direct material usage variance

> The difference between the standard cost of the material that should have been used and the standard cost of the material that was used

Example	
	£
1,000 units should have cost (× £50)	50,000
but did cost	46,075
Direct material total variance	3,925 (F)
	£
4,850 kg should have cost (× £10)	48,500
but did cost	46,075
Direct material price variance	2,425 (F)
1,000 units should have used (× 5 kg)	5,000 kg
but did use	4,850 kg
Variance in kg	150 kg (F)
× standard cost per kg	× £10
Direct material usage variance	£1,500 (F)

Direct labour total variance

The difference between what the output should have cost and what it actually cost, in terms of labour.

Again this can be divided into two sub-variances.

Direct labour rate variance

The difference between what the labour used should have cost and what it did cost

Direct labour efficiency variance

The difference between the standard cost of the hours that should have been worked and that standard cost of the hours that were worked. When idle time occurs, the efficiency variance is based on hours actually worked (not hours paid for) and an **idle time variance** (hours of idle time × standard rate per hour) is calculated.

Example

	£
1,000 units should have cost (× £20)	20,000
but did cost	21,210
Direct labour total variance	**1,210 (A)**

	£
4,200 hrs should have cost (× £5)	21,000
but did cost	21,210
Direct labour rate variance	**210 (A)**

1,000 units should have used	4,000 hrs
but did use	4,200 hrs
Variance in hours	200 hrs (A)
× standard rate per hour	× £5
Direct labour efficiency variance	**£1,000 (A)**

Variable overhead total variance

The difference between what the output should have cost and what it did cost, in terms of variable overhead

Variable overhead expenditure variance

The difference between the amount of variable overhead that should have been incurred and the amount that was actually incurred in the hours actively worked

Variable overhead efficiency variance

The difference between the standard cost of the hours that should have been worked and the standard cost of the hours that were worked

Example	
	£
1,000 units should have cost (× £8)	8,000
but did cost	9,450
Variable o/hd total variance	1,450 (A)
	£
4,200 hrs should have cost (× £2)	8,400
but did cost	9,450
Variable o/hd exp'd variance	1,050 (A)
Labour efficiency variance in hrs	200 hrs (A)
× standard rate per hour	× £2
Variable o/hd efficiency variance	£400 (A)

The total variance is the difference between fixed overhead incurred and fixed overhead absorbed (= under- or over-absorbed fixed overhead).

Expenditure variance

The difference between budgeted and actual fixed overhead expenditure

Example

	£
Budgeted o/hd (1,200 × £24)	28,800
Actual overhead	25,000
Expenditure variance	**3,800 (F)**

Over-absorbed part

Causes of under/over absorption

- Actual expenditure ≠ budgeted expenditure ⇒ expenditure variance
- Actual prod'n (units or hrs) ≠ budgeted prod'n ⇒ volume variance

Example

	£
Overhead incurred	25,000
Overhead absorbed (1,000 × £24)	24,000
Under-absorbed overhead/total variance	1,000 (A)*

Volume variance

The difference between actual and budgeted production units × standard absorption rate per unit

Example

	£
Actual prod'n at std rate (1,000 × £24)	24,000
Budgeted prod'n at std rate (1,200 × £24)	28,800
Volume variance	**4,800 (A)***

*(A) because actual output less than budgeted output

In a marginal costing system there is no volume variance.

The total fixed overhead variance is the difference between the overhead incurred and the overhead absorbed into the cost of production (= under- or over-absorbed overhead). There are two reasons why under or over absorption occur.

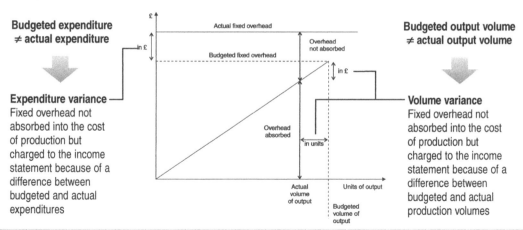

Budgeted expenditure ≠ actual expenditure

Expenditure variance
Fixed overhead not absorbed into the cost of production but charged to the income statement because of a difference between budgeted and actual expenditures

Budgeted output volume ≠ actual output volume

Volume variance
Fixed overhead not absorbed into the cost of production but charged to the income statement because of a difference between budgeted and actual production volumes

Selling (or sales) price variance

A measure of the effect on expected profit of a different selling price to standard

The difference between what the sales revenue should have been for the actual quantity sold, and what it was

Example

	£
Revenue from 900 units should have been (× £150)	135,000
but was (× £140)	126,000
Selling price variance	**9,000 (A)**

Don't forget to value the sales volume variance at standard contribution margin if marginal costing is in use.

The interdependence between the two variances should be clear.

Sales volume variance

A measure of the effect on expected profit of a different sales volume to that budgeted

The difference between the actual units sold and the budgeted quantity, valued at the standard profit per unit

Example

Budgeted sales volume	1,000 units
Actual sales volume	900 units
Variance in units	100 units (A)
× std profit margin per unit (× £(150 − 102))	× £48
Sales volume variance	**£4,800 (A)**

13a: Further variance analysis

Most common presentation (absorption costing)

	£	£
Budgeted profit		X
Sales variances – price	X	
– volume	X	
		X
Actual sales minus standard cost of sales		X

Cost variances	£ (F)	£ (A)	
Material price etc	X		
Fixed o/hd volume etc		X	
	X	X	X
Actual profit			X

Most common presentation (marginal costing)

	£	£
Budgeted profit		X
Budgeted fixed production overhead		X
Budgeted contribution		X
Sales variances (price and volume)		X
Actual sales minus std variable cost of sales		X
Variable cost variances		X
Actual contribution		X
Budgeted fixed production overhead	X	
Expenditure variance	X	
Actual fixed production overhead		X
Actual profit		X

Inventory adjustment

If actual sales volume $\neq$ actual production volume, and inventory is valued at actual cost, the difference between closing inventory valuations at actual cost and standard cost is added to the bottom of the operating statement.

One way of testing your understanding of variance analysis is to provide information about variances from which you have to 'work backwards' to determine the actual results.

This type of question really tests your understanding of the subject.

Example

Suppose we do not know the actual hours.

Total direct wages cost	£21,210
Less rate variance (given)	£210 (A)
Standard rate for actual hrs	£21,000
÷ standard rate per hr (given)	÷ £5
Actual hours worked	4,200 hrs

Example

Suppose we do not know the actual material used.

Let the number of kg purchased and used = x

	£
x kg should have cost (× £10)	10.0x
but did cost (× £9.50)	9.5x
Material price variance	0.5x (F)

Having been provided with the variance
(£2,425 (F)), you can calculate x = 2,425/0.5 = 4,850 kg

If a product requires two or more raw materials, and the proportions of the materials are changeable and controllable, the materials usage variance can be split into a mix variance and a yield variance.

Materials yield variance

A measure of the effect on costs of inputs yielding more or less than expected

Calculated as the difference between the expected output and the actual output, valued at the standard cost per unit of output

Calculating the yield variance

1. Find, for one unit of output, the standard *total* materials usage in kg, litres etc, and the cost of this standard usage.

2. Determine the standard output from the actual total quantity input.

Example

1. Std input to produce 1 unit of X:

A	20 kg × £10	£200
B	30 kg × £5	£150
	$\overline{50 \text{ kg}}$	$\overline{£350}$

In May, 13 units of X were produced from 250 kg of A and 350 kg of B.

2. (250+350) kg should have

yielded (÷ 50 kg)	12X
but did yield	$\overline{13X}$
Yield variance in units	$\overline{1X}$ (F)
× standard cost per unit of output	× £350
Yield variance in £	$\overline{£350}$ (F)

Materials mix variance

1. A measure of whether the actual mix is cheaper or more expensive than the standard

2. Calculated as the difference between the actual total quantity used in the standard mix and the actual quantity used in the actual mix, **valued** using one of two methods

   EITHER Standard input price of each material

   OR The difference between the standard weighted average price and the individual standard input prices

Calculating the mix variance

1. Calculate the standard mix of the actual materials used.

2. Find (in kg, litres etc for each input) the differences between what should have been used (step 1) and what was actually used.

3. Value the variances using one of the two methods.

You are only required to be able to calculate total mix variances. It therefore does not matter which of the valuation methods you use as the total variance is the same using both approaches. We recommend using the standard input price as it is slightly quicker.

13a: Further variance analysis

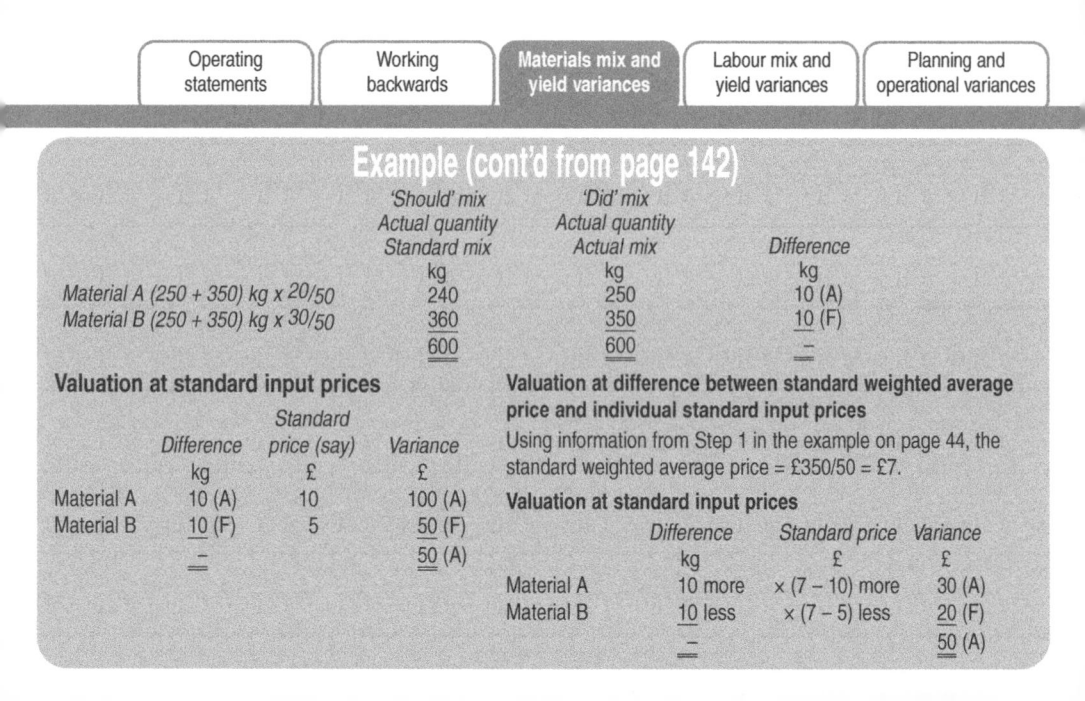

Example (cont'd from page 142)

	'Should' mix Actual quantity Standard mix kg	'Did' mix Actual quantity Actual mix kg	Difference kg
Material A (250 + 350) kg x 20/50	240	250	10 (A)
Material B (250 + 350) kg x 30/50	360	350	10 (F)
	600	600	—

Valuation at standard input prices

	Difference kg	Standard price (say) £	Variance £
Material A	10 (A)	10	100 (A)
Material B	10 (F)	5	50 (F)
	—		50 (A)

Valuation at difference between standard weighted average price and individual standard input prices

Using information from Step 1 in the example on page 44, the standard weighted average price = £350/50 = £7.

Valuation at standard input prices

	Difference kg	Standard price £	Variance £
Material A	10 more	× (7 − 10) more	30 (A)
Material B	10 less	× (7 − 5) less	20 (F)
	—		50 (A)

The total mix variance in quantity (here 10 kg (A) + 10 kg (F)) is always zero.

The total mix variance (in £) is the same by both methods.

Actual input of material compared with standard	Standard input price compared with weighted average price	Variance
More (A)	More	(A)
More (A)	Less	(F)
Less (F)	More	(F)
Less (F)	Less	(A)

The overall mix variance (in £) is adverse because more of the more expensive material was used than anticipated.

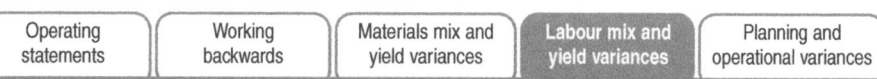

| Operating statements | Working backwards | Materials mix and yield variances | **Labour mix and yield variances** | Planning and operational variances |

Labour mix variance

- Also known as the **team composition variance**
- A measure of whether the actual mix of labour grades is cheaper or more expensive than the standard mix
- Calculated in exactly the same way as the materials mix variance

Labour yield variance

- Also known as the **team productivity variance**
- Shows how productively people are working
- Calculated in exactly the same way as the materials yield variance

Summary of direct labour cost variances

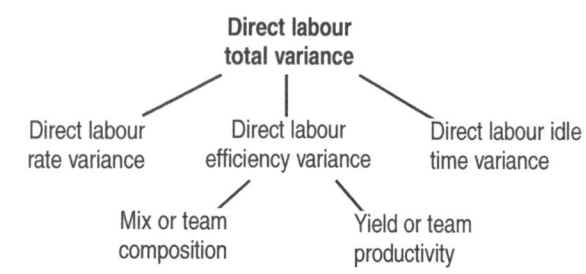

As with the materials mix variance, CIMA recommends two methods of valuing the labour mix variance.

Planning and operational variances

A **planning** variance arises because of **inaccurate planning** or **faulty standards**.

An **operational** variance compares **actual results** with the **revised** (or **ex-post**) **standard**.

If the original (ex-ante) standard is lower than the revised (ex-post) standard, the variance is adverse, and vice-versa.

Planning variance

Revised standard cost of actual production less: Original Standard cost of actual production.

 Follow-up action: better standard setting in the future

Operational variance

Revised standard cost of actual production less: Actual cost of actual production

Follow-up action: production/procurement management to take action as necessary

13a: Further variance analysis

Operational price/rate variance

Revised std price of actual purchase/hours paid (kg/hrs)	X
Actual price of actual purchases/hours paid (kg/hrs)	X
	X

Operational usage/efficiency variance

Actual output should have used	X	
But did use	X	
Operational usage variance in kg/hrs	X	kg/hrs
x revised std cost per kg/hr	£X	
	£X	

Planning price/rate variance

Original std cost for revised std kg/hrs for actual output	X
Revised std cost for revised std kg/hrs for actual output	X
	X

Planning usage/efficiency variance

Original std kg/hrs for actual output	X	
Revised std kg/hrs for actual output	X	
Planning usage variance in kg/hrs	X	kg/hrs
x std cost per kg/hr	£X	
	£X	

13b: Interpretation of variances

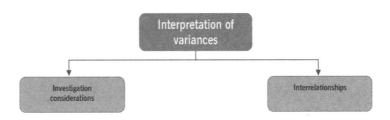

Variance	Favourable	Adverse
Material price	Unforeseen discounts received, greater care in purchasing	Price increase (inflation, seasonal variations, rush orders), careless purchasing
Material usage	Higher quality material, more effective use of material	Defective material, excessive waste, theft, stricter quality control
Labour rate	Use of workers with a lower rate of pay than standard	Unexpected overtime working (premium rate), productivity bonuses, rate increase
Idle time	Could occur if there is budgeted idle time	Machine breakdown, non-availability of material, illness or injury to worker

| Labour efficiency | Output produced more quickly than expected due to worker motivation, better quality equipment/materials | Lost time/down time/rest periods in excess of standard allowed, poor labour productivity due to lack of training, sub-standard materials, shorter batch runs |
| Overhead expenditure | Either the price component (eg salaries) or usage component (eg number of staff) can vary. | |

Do not just learn these causes by rote. You must be able to apply them to a scenario question.

In general, when deciding whether or not to investigate a particular variance, bear in mind six points.

- Materiality
- Controllability
- Variance trend ──────── Consider using % variance charts
- Costs v benefits
- Type of performance standard used
- Interdependence/interrelationship

Why might variances occur?

- Actual outcome measurement errors
- Out-of-date standards
- Inefficient or efficient operations
- Random or chance fluctuations (remember that standards are average)

The cause of one (adverse) variance may be wholly or partially explained by the cause of another (favourable) variance.

- Material price and usage variances
- Material price and labour efficiency variances
- Labour rate and efficiency variances
- Labour rate and material usage variances
- Sales price and volume variances
- Materials mix and yield variances

The significance of a variance can be assessed using a variance investigation model.

Reporting by exception

This involves deciding a limit, say 5%, and if a variance is within 5% of standard in any one period, it should be considered immaterial. Only if it exceeds the limit should it be considered materially significant and worthy of investigation.

Problems
■ Ignores trend in and past history of variances
■ Ignores costs/benefits
■ Ignores absolute materiality
■ Ignores sharp fluctuations within the limit set
■ Deciding on pre-set percentage
■ How to treat favourable and adverse variances

Some difficulties can be overcome by varying the pre-set percentage from account to account.

13b: Interpretation of variances

Statistical significance model

Historical data is used to calculate an expected average and the standard deviation of variation around this average when the process is under control (ie when variances are simply due to random fluctuations), on the assumption that the variances are normally distributed.

A variance will be investigated if it is more than an amount that the estimated normal distribution suggests is likely if the process is in control.

Example

A variance greater than 1.96 standard deviations from the mean has only a 2½% chance of happening under normal operating conditions. This is unusual and so such a variance should be investigated.

Advantages

- Important costs that normally vary by only a small amount from standard will be signalled for investigation if variances increase significantly.

- Costs that usually fluctuate by large amounts will not be signalled for investigation unless variances are extremely large.

The main disadvantage is the problem of assessing standard deviations.

Statistical control charts

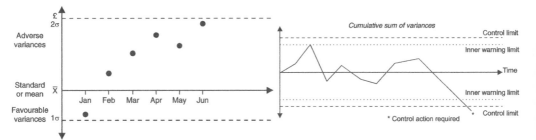

$\bar{x}$ control chart

£
2σ

Adverse
variances

Standard
or mean $\bar{x}$

Jan Feb Mar Apr May Jun

Favourable
variances
1σ

Cusum chart

Cumulative sum of variances

Control limit

Inner warning limit

Time

Inner warning limit

Control limit

* Control action required

Features of $\bar{x}$ control chart

- Limits are set at a certain number of standard deviations depending on the level of confidence required
- Highlights trends
- Identifies variances of such magnitude that they are unlikely to have arisen by chance

Features of cusum chart

- Shows cumulative sum of variances
- Trends detected earlier than when using $\bar{x}$ control chart

13b: Interpretation of variances

Benchmarking

'The establishment, through data gathering, of targets and comparators, through whose use relative levels of performance (and particularly areas of under-performance) can be identified. By the adoption of identified best practices it is hoped that performance will improve.' (CIMA)

Like standard costing, benchmarking is a comparison exercise through which an organisation attempts to improve performance.

Types of benchmarking

- **Internal.** Comparing the performance of one operating unit or function with another in the same industry

- **Functional/operational/generic.** Comparing performance of an internal function with the best external practitioners of the function, regardless of the industry

- **Competitive.** Comparing performance with direct competitors (using, for example, reverse engineering)

- **Strategic.** Type of competitive benchmarking aimed at strategic action and organisational change

Obtaining information

Financial information about competitors is easier to acquire than non-financial information.

Information about products can be obtained from reverse engineering, product literature, media comment and trade associations.

Information about processes is more difficult to find. Such information can be obtained from group companies or non-competing organisations in the same industry.

Advantages

- An effective method of implementing change

- Flexible (can be used in private and public sectors and by staff at different levels of responsibility)

- Cross comparisons are more likely to expose radical new ways of doing things

- Establishes a desire for continuous improvement

Benchmarking and standards

Benchmarking allows attainable standards to be set. 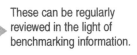 These can be regularly reviewed in the light of benchmarking information. They then become part of a programme of continuous improvement by becoming increasingly demanding.

13b: Interpretation of variances

Notes

14: Risk and uncertainty in decision making

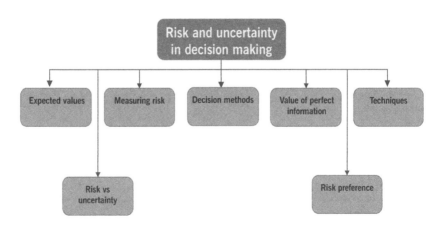

Risk

Involves situations or events which may or may not occur, but whose probability of occurrence can be calculated statistically and the frequency of their occurrence predicted from past records.

Uncertainty

Involves events whose outcome *cannot* be predicted with statistical confidence.

An event will be risky or uncertain depending on whether or not sufficient information is available to allow the lack of certainty to be quantified. As a rule, however, the terms are used interchangeably.

Attitude to risk

Risk seeker   A decision maker interested in the best outcomes no matter how small the chance that they may occur

Risk neutral   A decision maker concerned with what will be the most likely outcome

Risk averse   A decision maker who acts on the assumption that the worst outcome might occur

The risk of a particular course of action should be considered in the context of the overall 'portfolio' of strategies adopted by an organisation.

Expected values (EV)

The EV of an opportunity is equal to the sum of (the probability of an outcome occurring × the return expected if it does occur) = Σpx (where p = probability of an outcome occurring and x = value of that outcome).

The calculation of EVs is more useful as a decision-making technique when outcomes will occur many times over (for example, the calculation of expected sales levels on the basis of sales levels over 360 previous days) rather than when a decision must be made once only (such as an investment decision based on a 70% chance of a profit of £50,000 and a 30% chance of a loss of £70,000).

Example

If contribution could be £10,000, £20,000 or £30,000 with respective probabilities of 0.3, 0.5 and 0.2, the EV of contribution =

	£
£10,000 × 0.3	3,000
£20,000 × 0.5	10,000
£30,000 × 0.2	6,000
EV of contribution	19,000

There may be additional conditions, for example there may be only a 75% chance of making one of these three positive contributions and a 25% chance of a negative contribution of £10,000, in which case the EV = (£19,000 (calculation above) × 0.75) − (£10,000 × 0.25) = £14,250 − £2,500 = £11,750.

Bayes' strategy

When faced with a number of alternative decisions each with a range of possible outcomes, the optimum decision will be the one which gives the highest EV.

Joint/combined probabilities

Example

If there is a 40% chance that costs will be £8 and a 75% probability that sales will be 500 units, the joint/combined probability of these two events is $0.4 \times 0.75 = 0.3$ and if other probabilities are £10 (60%) and 1,000 units (25%), the information can be tabulated as follows.

Volume	Prob	Cost	Prob	Combined Prob	Total cost £	EV of total cost £
500	0.75	£8	0.4	0.30	4,000	1,200
		£10	0.6	0.45	5,000	2,250
1,000	0.25	£8	0.4	0.10	8,000	800
		£10	0.6	0.15	10,000	1,500
				1.00		5,750

Cumulative probabilities

In the example opposite the cumulative probability that, say, total cost will be less than £10,000 is the sum of the combined probabilities for any total cost figure below £10,000 = 0.3 + 0.45 + 0.1 = 0.85.

Data tables

One-way/two-way data tables show the effects of a range of values of one/two variables.

Example

The spreadsheet shows an input section (cells A1 to B3), a combined calculation and output section (cells A6 to B8), and a two-way data table showing the profit earned at different combinations of sales volume (cells B10 to D10) and price (cells A11 to A13) (eg 750 x £(8 – 5) = £2,250).

	A	B	C	D
1	Price	£10.00		
2	Cost	£5.00		
3	Volume	1,000 units		
4				
5		£		
6	Sales	10,000		
7	Costs	(5,000)		
8	Profit	5,000		
9				
10	=B8	750	1,000	1,250
11	8	2,250	3,000	3,750
12	10	3,750	5,000	6,250
13	12	5.250	7,000	8,750
14				

Maximin, maximax and minimax regret

Decision makers may base their decisions on choices other than highest expected profit.

- Playing safe – maximin
- Best outcome whatever the likelihood – maximax
- Opportunity loss – minimax regret

Using the standard deviation to measure risk

$$s = \sqrt{\Sigma p(x - \overline{x})^2} = \sqrt{\text{variance}}$$

where $\overline{x}$ is the EV of the variable in question, x is each possible value of the variable and p is the probability of each possible variable value.

Risk can be measured by the possible variations of outcomes around the EV using the standard deviation, s. Risks can be compared using the coefficient of variation (s ÷ EV of variable in question).

Preparation

1   Always work **chronologically** from **left to right.**

2   Start with a (labelled) **decision point.**

3   Add branches for each option/alternative.

4   If the outcome of an option is 100% certain, the branch for that alternative is complete.

5   If the outcome of an option is uncertain (because there are a number of possible outcomes), add an **outcome point.**

6   For each possible outcome, add a branch (with the relevant probability) to the outcome point.

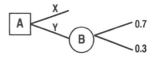

Evaluating the decision

Work from **right to left** and calculate the EV of revenue/cost/contribution/profit at each outcome point (**rollback analysis**).

Example

As a result of an increase in demand for a town's car parking facilities, the owners of a car park are reviewing their business operations. A decision has to be made now to select one of the following three options for the next year.

Option 1: Make no change. Annual profit is £100,000. There is little likelihood that this will provoke new competition this year.

Option 2: Raise prices by 50%. If this occurs there is a 75% chance that an entrepreneur will set up in competition this year. The Board's estimate of its annual profit in this situation would be as follows.

2A WITH a new competitor		2B WITHOUT a new competitor	
Probability	Profit	Probability	Profit
0.7	£120,000	0.3	£150,000
0.3	£150,000	0.7	£200,000

Option 3: Expand the car park quickly, at a cost of £50,000, keeping prices the same. The profits are then estimated to be like 2B above, except that the probabilities would be 0.6 and 0.4 respectively.

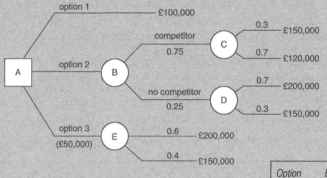

At C, expected profit = (150 × 0.3) + (120 × 0.7) = £129,000
At D, expected profit = (200 × 0.7) + (150 × 0.3) = £185,000
At B, expected profit = (129 × 0.75) + (185 × 0.25) = £143,000
At E, expected profit = (200 × 0.6) + (150 × 0.4) = £180,000

Option	Expected profit
	£'000
1	100
2	143
3 (180 – 50)	130

The value of perfect information

1 Work out the EVs of all options and see which is best.

2 See what decision would be taken with perfect information (if all the outcomes were known in advance with certainty) and calculate the EV.

3 The value of perfect information (the amount you would be willing to pay to obtain it) = EV of the action you would take with the information – EV without the information.

Alternatively a decision tree can be used.

Example

	Profit if strong demand	Profit/(loss) if weak demand
Option A	£4,000	£(1,000)
Option B	£1,500	£600
Probability	0.3	0.7

EV of A = $4,000 \times 0.3 + (1,000) \times 0.7 = £500$

EV of B = $1,500 \times 0.3 + 600 \times 0.7 = £870$

∴ Choose B

With perfect information, if demand is strong choose A but if demand is weak choose B.

∴ EV with perfect information = $0.3 \times 4,000 + 0.7 \times 600$

= £1,620

∴ Value of perfect information = $£(1,620 - 870)$

= £750

Example

X Co is trying to decide whether or not to build a shopping centre. The probability that the centre will be successful based on past experience is 0.6.

X Co could conduct market research to help with the decision.

- If the centre is going to be successful there is a 75% chance that the market research will say so.
- If the centre is not going to be successful there is a 95% chance that the survey will say so.

The information can be tabulated as follows.

		Actual			
		Success	Failure	Total	
Research	Success	** 45	2	47	* given
	Failure	*** 15	38	53	** 0.75 × 60
Total		* 60	40	100	*** balancing figure

The probabilities are as follows.

P (research says success)	= 0.47
P (research says failure)	= 0.53

If the survey says success

P (success)	= 45/47	= 0.957
P (failure)	= 2/47	= 0.043

If the survey says failure

P (success)	= 15/53	= 0.283
P (failure)	= 38/53	= 0.717

The essence of all approaches to sensitivity analysis is to carry out calculations with one set of values for the variables and then substitute other possible values for the variables to see how this affects the overall outcome.

Approach 3

Estimate by how much a variable would need to differ before a decision maker was indifferent between two options.

Approach 1
Estimate by how much a variable would need to differ from its estimated value before the decision would change.

Sensitivity analysis is one form of 'what-if?' analysis

Approach 2
Estimate whether a decision would change if a variable was X% higher or lower than expected.

Example

Option 2 is £10,000 more expensive than option 1 and involves taking a discount of 10% from a supplier from whom you purchase £50,000 of goods (before discount) pa for 4 years. Ignore the time value of money. Discount needs to be £10,000 (difference) + £20,000 (current discount) if option 2 is as good as option 1.

$\therefore \ (4 \times £50,000) \times X\% = £30,000$

$\therefore \ X = 15\%$ (rate at which you are indifferent between the two options)

Monte Carlo method

1. Identify the probabilities of particular variable values occurring.

2. Allocate a range of numbers to each possible variable value in proportion to the probabilities.

   - Probability to 1 decimal place → 10 numbers (0-9)
     Probability to 2 decimal places → 100 numbers (00-99) and so on

   - A probability of 0.15 gets 0.15 of the total numbers to be assigned, that is 15 numbers: (00, 01, 02, 03, ..., 14)

3. Run the simulation model so that random numbers are generated (either manually or by a computer).

4. Allocate variable values on the basis of the generated random numbers.

Example

Daily demand	Probability	Numbers assigned
Units		
17	0.15	00-14
18	0.45	15-59
19	0.40	60-99
	1.00	

Random numbers for a simulation over three days are 761301.

Day	Random number	Demand
1	76	19
2	13	17
3	01	17

Learning curve theory

This is used to measure how the incremental cost per unit of output continues to fall for each extra unit produced.

$$Y_x = aX^b$$

Example

The value of b for a 70% learning curve

$$= \frac{\log 0.7}{\log 2}$$

$$= \frac{-0.1590}{0.3010}$$

$$= -0.515$$

b = learning coefficient = $\dfrac{\log \text{ of learning rate}}{\log \text{ of } 2}$

a = time required to produce the first unit of output

X = cumulative number of units

Y = cumulative average time per unit to produce X units

Notes

Notes

Notes

Notes

Notes

Notes

Notes